MW01119172

THE NEW,
DYNAMIC
CHURCH

Other books by Victor Paul Wierwille

Receiving the Holy Spirit Today
Are the Dead Alive Now?
Studies in Abundant Living Series
   Volume I, *The Bible Tells Me So*
   Volume III, *The Word's Way*
   Volume IV, *God's Magnified Word*
   Volume V, *Order My Steps in Thy Word*
Jesus Christ Is Not God
Jesus Christ Our Passover
Jesus Christ Our Promised Seed

THE NEW, DYNAMIC CHURCH

Volume II
Studies in Abundant Living

Victor Paul Wierwille

American Christian Press
The Way International
New Knoxville, Ohio 45871

The scriptures used throughout this book are quoted from the King James Version unless otherwise noted. All explanatory insertions by the author within a scripture verse are enclosed in brackets. All Greek and Hebrew words are printed with English letters and italicized.

International Standard Book Number 0-910068-82-8
Library of Congress Catalog Card Number 99-96337
American Christian Press
The Way International
New Knoxville, Ohio 45871

To my son
John Paul Wierwille

NOTE TO THE READER

As a workman of God's Word, Dr. Victor Paul Wierwille continued to grow in knowledge and understanding, striving always to rightly divide the Word of Truth. Readers can enjoy the further research on topics found in Volumes I through V of Studies in Abundant Living that Dr. Wierwille incorporated in *Receiving the Holy Spirit Today, Are the Dead Alive Now?, Jesus Christ Is Not God, Jesus Christ Our Passover,* and *Jesus Christ Our Promised Seed.*

CONTENTS

PREFACE

The New, Dynamic Church is organized into five parts: "The Dynamic Church," "A Christian's Birth and Growth," "A Christian's Power Base," "The Church Today," and "Living the Word." Within each part are chapters, each chapter having been researched and originally written as an individual study. By loosely grouping the studies into general topics, a person can get a broader perspective as the parts fit together to make up the larger whole.

However, because the chapters were written as individual studies and then put into topical units, occasionally a reader may find that all facets of the topic are not covered; however, they have been covered in other research writings. I know the contents of Volume II of Studies in Abundant Living will not only open up more of God's Word for you, but will also uplift you—mentally and physically and spiritually.

Let us put God's Word in our hearts and minds, for it alone can give us complete deliverance from the darkness of this world.

PART I

THE DYNAMIC
CHURCH

PART I

THE DYNAMIC CHURCH

The word "dynamic" in the above title has a double meaning. "Dynamic" primarily denotes the ability to change; dynamic is in direct contrast to static, which shows inertia or sameness.

During several administrations, God ordained that His people be organized in the *ekklēsia,* the church, the called-out. The *ekklēsia* of Israel is Biblically called the bride of Christ, while the *ekklēsia* of Grace is called the Body of Christ. So much error has come about by confusing these two distinct, separate churches that a careful study of both the church of Israel and the Church of Grace is certainly needed.

The dynamic church is the changed, changing church. God's plan for the church of Israel was carried out during the age of Law and during Jesus Christ's presence on earth. However, the *ekklēsia* of Israel has been temporarily suspended since the day of Pentecost. We are living during the age of the *ekklēsia* of Grace. But someday when this Age of Grace is terminated with the return of Christ, the *ekklēsia* of Israel will be reestablished.

3

Historically the church has been dynamic not only in changing from one administration to the next, but also in the power which God has given it. In order to be most effective in using our God-given power, we as members of the Church first must have knowledge of His will, which is stated in His Word. We, too, then can be dynamic; this is, having the ability to change and effectively meet every new and different situation with God's effectual power.

Chapter One

EKKLĒSIA: BRIDE OR BODY?

Bible commentaries and Biblical writers frequently refer to both the church of the Gospels and the Church of the Epistles as the bride of Christ, thus making the two usages synonymous. Thus the relationship of Christ to the church of the Gospels and to the church of the Book of Revelation in contrast to the Church of the Epistles has not been properly understood. The Word of God separates these two bodies, with the bride of Christ being the church of the Gospels and the Body of Christ being the Church of the Epistles.

But before we begin a study of the significance of the two churches, let's examine what we mean by the word "church."

When we see a building with a steeple on it, we point to it and say, "That is a church." This is one usage—a building. Another current usage of "church" is a group of people who gather for religious ritual. We also refer to various denominations such as the Methodist, Presbyterian, or Roman Catholic as churches. Another usage of the word "church" is a group of people who are born again of God's Spirit. The meaning of "church" varies with its context.

The Greek word for our English word "church" is *ekklēsia,* meaning "the called-out." People may be called out for various reasons; for example, if a group of people decided they were going bowling and then gathered at the bowling alley, they would be an *ekklēsia* because they are *called out* to bowl. In Acts 19 a mob is called a church, an *ekklēsia.* Why? Because a mob is composed of a group of people who have gathered for a specific purpose.

> Acts 19:23-32:
> And the same time there arose no small stir about that way.
>
> For a certain *man* named Demetrius, a silversmith, which made silver shrines for Diana, brought no small gain unto the craftsmen;
>
> Whom he called together with the workmen of like occupation, and said, Sirs, ye know that by this craft we have our wealth.

Moreover ye see and hear, that not alone at Ephesus, but almost throughout all Asia, this Paul hath persuaded and turned away much people, saying that they be no gods, which are made with hands:

So that not only this our craft is in danger to be set at nought; but also that the temple of the great goddess Diana should be despised, and her magnificence should be destroyed, whom all Asia and the world worshippeth.

And when they heard *these sayings* [of Demetrius], they were full of wrath, and cried out, saying, Great *is* Diana of the Ephesians.

And the whole city was filled with confusion: and having caught Gaius and Aristarchus, men of Macedonia, Paul's companions in travel, they rushed with one accord into the theatre.

And when Paul would have entered in unto the people, the disciples suffered him not.

And certain of the chief of Asia, which were his friends, sent unto him, desiring *him* that he would not adventure himself into the theatre.

> Some therefore cried one thing, and some
> another: for the assembly [*ekklēsia,* the
> church] was confused; and the more part
> knew not wherefore they were come
> together.

A large company of silversmiths under
Demetrius were stirred up for fear that their
comfortable income was being diminished by
Paul's coming to town. Paul preached the greatness of God's Word, which is against the usage
of medals, amulets, and charms to represent God
and His blessings. Although the mob wasn't certain what the real issue was, Demetrius had emo-
tionally incited them against Paul. One group
cried one thing and some another because the
church, the assembly, the *ekklēsia,* was confused.
"And the more part knew not wherefore they
were come together." This is a mob—following
along with the confused assemblage. The word
"assembly" in Acts 19 is *ekklēsia,* church, the
called-out.

The *ekklēsia* or the called-out of Israel, the
bride of Christ, covers the time span of the
Gospels. Jesus Christ came unto Israel, his own
people. This era of the *ekklēsia* of the bride is
called the Kingdom of Heaven because the king
from heaven was on earth.

Before we go further, it is necessary to clarify the difference between the Kingdom of Heaven and the Kingdom of God. The Kingdom of God has no beginning and no ending. The Kingdom of God spans all existence. However, under this all-expansive Kingdom of God are several periods, one of which is the Kingdom of Heaven. The Kingdom of Heaven period is for the called-out of Israel, the church of Israel, which is the bride of Christ. Each time the Kingdom of Heaven is referred to, the personal presence of the king himself upon earth is designated.

USAGE OF THE WORD "CHURCH"
ekklēsia — CALLED OUT

━━━ KINGDOM OF GOD ━━━

ekklēsia ISRAEL	*ekklēsia* JEW (JUDEAN) AND GENTILE	*ekklēsia* ISRAEL
BRIDE OF CHRIST KINGDOM OF HEAVEN KING DOM — REIGN	BODY OF CHRIST THE GREAT MYSTERY	BRIDE & BRIDEGROOM KINGDOM OF HEAVEN KING DOM — REIGN
LAW GOSPELS	GRACE CHURCH EPISTLES ── HELD IN ABEYANCE ──	LAW BOOK OF REVELATION

9

The word "kingdom" is made up of two words: *king* and *dom, dom* meaning "reign or supremacy." Therefore, "kingdom" means "the rulership of a king." There cannot be a kingdom without a king. Great Britain can speak of itself as a kingdom because of the reign of a king or a queen. Citizens of the United States of America cannot speak of their land as a kingdom, for there is no monarch. While Jesus Christ was on earth, it was his reign. During his reign he called out those people of Israel who believed in him as the Messiah. Not only did Jesus himself minister to the people of Israel, but he also sent the twelve apostles to the lost sheep of the house of Israel. When Jesus sent out the seventy, he directed them also to the lost sheep of the house of Israel. He told them *not* to go unto the Gentiles because Jesus had come unto God's own, Israel, and called out from Israel those who were to make up the bride. Jesus Christ was the bridegroom. The church, the called-out of Israel, was called the bride while the bridegroom was on the earth.

But what happened to the bridegroom? He was nailed to the cross. When the king of the kingdom was crucified, the church as the bride was interrupted because the bridegroom was dead. As previously noted, God promised that there would be no end to the Kingdom of Heaven,* but man killed the king. What happened to God's promise? God promised that when the king came he would build the church, and the gates of hell would not prevail against it. But when the king was crucified, the bridegroom was dead, and it appeared that the kingdom had been defeated. However, this is not so, for the Church of the Bride is yet to be fulfilled in the future. The same church referred to in Revelation is again the Church of the Bride, just as it was in the Gospels.**

With the death of the king, the Kingdom of Heaven was interrupted; but God raised Jesus Christ from the dead, and he is coming back to earth. When Jesus Christ returns, he will not be born in a stable and laid in a manger. He is not coming to be mocked and nailed to a cross. Man is not going to spit in his face and press a crown of thorns on his head. When Jesus Christ comes again, he is coming as king of kings and lord of lords. The kingdom of the church of Israel is being held in abeyance until these events come

---

*Luke 1:33: "And he shall reign over the house of Jacob for ever; and of his kingdom there shall be no end."

**The church described and spoken of in the Book of Revelation has nothing to do with our time and our administration.

11

to pass. Then the bride and the bridegroom will be together again, and the "gates of hell shall not prevail against it [the Kingdom of Heaven]." It will then again be in effect. But in the meantime, while the bridegroom is gone, a different arrangement has been made. The next verse of Ephesians 1 explains what the Church with Christ as the head is.

> Ephesians 1:23:
> Which [the Church] is his body, the fulness of him that filleth all in all.

While the bridegroom is absent, the members of the Church make up the Body of Christ. In this Church of the Body, there is only one head, and that is the Lord Jesus Christ.

The Church of the Body, which in this Administration of Grace is the Church of Grace, is also called the Church of God.* Jesus came to fulfill

---

*Ephesians 1:22 and 23: "And hath put all *things* under his feet, and gave him *to be* the head over all *things* to the church, Which is his body, the fulness of him that filleth all in all."

Ephesians 3:2: "If ye have heard of the dispensation of the grace of God which is given me to you-ward."

I Corinthians 1:2: "Unto the church of God which is at Corinth, to them that are sanctified in Christ Jesus, called *to be* saints, with all that in every place call upon the name of Jesus Christ our Lord, both theirs and ours."

the law and to make the Church of Grace available. When all things were ready, the Church of Grace was founded, and the new birth was made available. From the day of Pentecost until the return of Christ, everyone who is born again of God's Spirit is a member of the Church of Grace, the Body of Christ. The membership of this Church of the Body consists of all those called out from among both Judean and Gentile. Therefore, any Judean or Gentile who confesses Jesus as his lord and believes that God raised him from the dead becomes a member of the Body of Christ.

Although believers on Pentecost received the new birth, the power from on high, they could not explain nor comprehend the fullness of the miracle which had occurred, just as I cannot explain electricity although I enjoy the utilization of it. On the day of Pentecost, and for a period of time following, the believers benefited from the new birth and the power from the Holy Spirit, but they could not explain what they had. Finally, years later, the revelation to explain the gift that came on Pentecost was given to the Apostle Paul. To Paul was revealed the greatest mystery the world has ever known—the mystery of the Body of Christ, which is his Church.

13

To discover when the Mystery was revealed to Paul, let us check Romans 16 and Ephesians 3.

Romans 16:25 and 26:
Now to him that is of power to stablish you according to my gospel, and the preaching of Jesus Christ, according to the revelation of the mystery, which was kept secret since the world began,

But now is made manifest, and by the scriptures of the prophets [not the Old Testament prophets, but the post-Pentecost prophets, who are members of the Church, the Body], according to the commandment of the everlasting God, made known to all nations for the obedience of faith.

Ephesians 3:2-5:
If ye have heard of the dispensation [or the administration] of the grace of God which is given me to you-ward:

How that by revelation he made known unto me the mystery; (as I wrote afore in few words,

Whereby, when ye read, ye may understand my knowledge in the mystery of Christ)

Which in other ages was not made known unto the sons of men, as it is now revealed unto his holy apostles and prophets by the Spirit.

The founding of the Church of the Body was not made known in other ages; thus the prophets of the Old Testament did not know about the Church of Grace; neither did the people living at the time of the Gospels. But it is "now [lately] revealed unto his holy apostles and prophets by the Spirit."

Once the timing of the revelation of the Mystery is clear, the essential question remains: What *is* the Mystery?

Ephesians 3:6:
That the Gentiles should be fellowheirs, and of the same body, and partakers of his promise in Christ by the gospel.

It was no mystery that the Gentiles would be blessed under Abraham's and David's ministries and during Israel's reign. Examples of the Gentiles' being blessed are scattered throughout the Old Testament. But the Old Testament does not give the slightest inkling that the Gentiles would ever be fellow heirs or joint heirs "of the

15

same body, and partakers of his promise in Christ by the gospel." The revelation of the Gentiles being fellow heirs in Christ was, to say the least, revolutionary news.

> Ephesians 3:7 and 8:
> Whereof I was made a minister, according to the gift of the grace of God given unto me by the effectual working of his power.
>
> Unto me, who am less than the least of all saints, is this grace given, that I should preach among the Gentiles the unsearchable riches of Christ.

The word "unsearchable" can be translated "untrackable." The mystery of the riches of God's grace to the Gentiles could literally not be tracked in the Word of God from the Old Testament through the Gospels. That the Gentiles should be fellow heirs and of the same Body was a secret, hidden from the beginning of the world.

> Ephesians 3:9:
> And to make all *men* see what *is* the fellowship of the mystery, which from the beginning of the world hath been hid in God, who created all things....

The revelation was made known "to make all *men* see what *is* the fellowship of the mystery." The word "fellowship" in the Greek text is the word "administration." The "fellowship of the mystery" is literally the "Administration of the Church of Grace."

> Colossians 1:26 and 27:
> *Even* the mystery which hath been hid from ages and from generations, but now is made manifest to his saints:
>
> To whom God would make known what *is* the riches of the glory of this mystery among the Gentiles; which is Christ in you, the hope of glory.

The Mystery, so important that it was kept secret since the foundation of the world, is that all born-again believers, Judeans and Gentiles, would be fellow heirs with Christ and that Christ would be *in* every one of them. Imagine that! When Jesus Christ was here upon earth, he could only be at one place at one time. But after he ascended into heaven, and God had given the power of the holy spirit on the day of Pentecost, then Christ could be in every born-again believer. Wherever a believer is, there Christ is present. Had the Devil known this mystery he would never have crucified Jesus. Through Jesus' death, resurrection, and ascension, power hitherto unknown in history was made available. The Devil was totally unaware of God's plan, as told in I Corinthians.

> I Corinthians 2:7 and 8:
> But we speak the wisdom of God in a mystery, *even* the hidden *wisdom,* which God ordained before the world unto our glory:
>
> Which none of the princes of this world knew: for had they known *it,* they would not have crucified the Lord of glory.

The Devil as ruling prince would much rather have had Jesus Christ personally present on earth than to have thousands of believers with *Christ in* them scattered across the world. By crucifying the lord of glory, Satan brought an unsolvable problem to himself.

Obviously the Devil was not the only one who was ignorant of the intentions of God. Many men before the time of the Church of Grace tried to find out about this period. Peter told of the Old Testament prophets' quests.

I Peter 1:10 and 11:

Of which salvation the prophets have inquired and searched diligently, who prophesied of the grace *that should come* unto you:

Searching what, or what manner of time the Spirit of Christ which was in them did signify, when it testified beforehand the sufferings of Christ, and the glory that should follow.

The literal translation according to usage of verse 11 reads: "Searching out unto the time of the spirit which was upon them did signify of Christ when it testified beforehand the sufferings of Christ, and the glory that should follow."

These Old Testament prophets diligently searched the Word for the time lapse between the Gospels and the Book of Revelation, between the suffering of Christ and his glory. But this period of grace could not be found because it was completely hidden.

The period of grace is indicated by Jesus' reading of Isaiah 61, which is recorded in Luke.

Luke 4:16:
And he [Jesus] came to Nazareth, where he
had been brought up: and, as his custom
was, he went into the synagogue on the sabbath day, and stood up for to read.

A wise and interesting tradition in the synagogues at the time was that whenever a man
read from the Word of God, he always stood to
show respect for the sacred scrolls and to show
that he was reading, not just talking on his own.
When a person finished reading the Word of
God and began teaching or discussing, the man
sat down. When a man sat, listeners were not
certain that the man ministering to them was
giving the Word; but when the minister was
standing and reading, the congregation knew that
they were hearing the Word of God. This is why
Jesus stood to read.

Luke 4:17:
And there was delivered unto him the book
[scroll] of the prophet Esaias [Isaiah]. And
when he had opened the book, he found the
place where it was written.

How thoroughly Jesus must have studied the
scroll of Isaiah! Although he did not have the

help of chapters and verses or center references, he "opened the book, [and] he found the place where it was written."

There is a story told of a man who said that he did not have to study the Bible to learn its message for him. All he had to do to find God's guidance each morning was to flip through the Bible and, while covering his eyes, place his finger on a verse. The verse on which his finger landed was his guidance for the day. An interesting guidance was given to this man one morning as he casually flipped to a page in the New Testament. He placed his finger on a verse, opened his eyes, and read, "And Judas went and hanged himself." The man was dissatisfied with this guidance, so he flipped to another page, and this time read, "Go, and do thou likewise." Shocked, the man gave his method a third try only to read, "That which thou doest, do quickly."

In contrast to this fellow, Jesus found the place where it was written; he deliberately located the scripture he needed at that particular time. Jesus was prepared, as Luke 4 demonstrates.

Luke 4:18-21:

The Spirit of the Lord *is* upon me, because he hath anointed me to preach the gospel to the poor; he hath sent me to heal the brokenhearted, to preach deliverance to the captives, and recovering of sight to the blind, to set at liberty them that are bruised,

To preach the acceptable year of the Lord.

And he closed the book, and he gave *it* again to the minister, and sat down. And the eyes of all them that were in the synagogue were fastened on him.

And he began to say unto them, This day is this scripture fulfilled in your ears.

Jesus stopped reading with the phrase, "to preach the acceptable year of the Lord," and sat down saying, "This day is this scripture fulfilled in your ears." Compare Luke 4 with Isaiah 61 from which Jesus read.

Isaiah 61:2:

To proclaim the acceptable year of the Lord, and the day of vengeance of our God....

Isaiah says, "To proclaim the acceptable year of the Lord, and the day of vengeance of our

God," but Jesus never read the last eight words. Why did he stop in the middle of the phrase? Had Jesus read the words "the day of vengeance of our God," and then said, "This day is this scripture fulfilled," Jesus would have been in error. Jesus could not say, "This day is the day of vengeance of our God fulfilled in your ears," because the day of vengeance had not yet come. The "day of vengeance of our God" will be fulfilled with the prophecy of Revelation when Christ will return as king of kings and lord of lords with all the power of God.

Jesus accurately divided the Word of God. Jesus Christ was to preach the acceptable year of the Lord—it was fulfilled. The day of vengeance had not yet come. In Isaiah 61:2 a comma is placed after the expression "to preach the acceptable year of the Lord," while in Luke 4:19 a period follows the same statement. The comma in Isaiah 61:2 represents all the years from the day of Pentecost until the time the Lord Jesus Christ will come again. The intervening time is the period of Grace, the Church to which post-Pentecost believers belong, which was still a mystery at the time of the writing of Isaiah and was unknown to Jesus.

The time of the Church of Grace is the day of man's judgment.

> I Corinthians 4:3:
> But with me it is a very small thing that I should be judged of you, or of man's judgment....

The words "man's judgment" are "Man's Day." Man does the judging today during the Age of Grace, for it is Man's Day. If this were not so, a man would not be able to curse God, use His name in vain, nor live like the Devil himself. In this Age of Grace man is free, but there is another judgment coming, as Revelation indicates.

> Revelation 1:10:
> I was in the Spirit on the Lord's day....

What exactly is the Lord's Day? Some people speak loosely of the Lord's Day as Sunday, yet for another group of people the Lord's Day is the Sabbath, Saturday. Biblically speaking, the Lord's Day has nothing to do with the day of the week. The Lord's Day is the age in which the lord does the judging. In that age nobody will nail him to a cross, nobody will curse him, nobody will mock him, for his return as king of kings will usher in the age of the vengeance of God spoken of in Isaiah 61.

To live in this Age of Grace, an age which was kept secret from the foundation of the world until it was revealed to Paul, is a tremendous privilege. Man has power and status in Christ which no other age has ever known.

The Church of the Bride did not know of the Church of Grace that was to come. The Church of Grace, the Church of the Body, was founded after the Church of the Bride was suspended at the time of the crucifixion and death of the bridegroom. The Church of the Bride will remain in that state until Christ returns. In the meantime, during the period of the Church of the Body, all believers are one in Christ Jesus, the head of that Body. Each born-again believer has Christ in him, the hope of glory. No other age has had this potential power for manifesting the greatness of God as have members of the Church of Grace. We must not allow this power of Christ in us to remain dormant. Now that Christ is in us spiritually, let us put on his mind and show forth our power to defeat the Devil and his forces of evil. We are more than conquerors *now*! We *now* have Christ in us, and we are *now* fellow heirs with him.

PART II

A Christian's
Birth and Growth

PART II

A Christian's Birth and Growth

In order to become a member of an earthly family, a person must first be born. Likewise, in order to be a member of God's heavenly family, a person must also have birth into God's family. In both cases we begin as babies. In the human family, a baby matures step-by-step, day by day. However, in God's family it takes more than just time for a baby to mature. In fact, some babies in Christ never mature—for two possible reasons: first, they may never have been taught or never have learned any more than how to be born into the family or, second, they may have rejected the plan of development which must be carried out if they are to spiritually mature. Maturity doesn't just happen spontaneously as a simple act of God.

In this part on "A Christian's Birth and Growth," we study God's Word to learn about our Christian development. This study eradicates the first problem of ignorance. The next step—applying God's plan for our spiritual growth—remains in our hands.

"The Unqualified Commitment" and "How to Be a Christian" show the foundational step of being born into the family of God. "Your Power of Attorney" and "Key to Power" tell of the rights and privileges we have as members of that family.

To this point we ourselves have done nothing to obtain what we have as sons of God. God in Christ did the work of giving us salvation and sonship rights. After spiritual birth with its inherent potential power, however, we must follow God's plan if we are going to outgrow our Christian "baby stage." We must apply our power of attorney and the other legal rights we have been given. "Fellowship Is the Secret" reveals the strength we have when we keep in fellowship and communion with God. "What Is True Worship?" studies what the Word says is worship. Worship according to the Bible has nothing to do with a church building or altars or candelabra. Worship is communion with God by way of the holy spirit. This truth answers a question which has been perplexing many people for a long time, and it enlightens our minds so that we know how God expects us to worship Him.

The final chapter in this part, "A Christian's Birth and Growth," shows the mature Christian in full bloom. We learned of the investment God puts within us at our birth as a Christian. Then we found that as we grow we cultivate that initial investment by staying in fellowship and by worshiping God by the spirit. When we as Christians are ready to accept "The Believer's Responsibility," it shows that we have progressed beyond the early self-focused stage. The Christian has spiritually matured to the point of accepting his responsibility which, simply stated, is to bear witness to the greatness of God and His Word to those who do not know. Then it is their decision to accept or reject birth and growth in God's family.

Chapter Two

THE UNQUALIFIED COMMITMENT

Romans 10 contains the unqualified commitment.

> Romans 10:9 and 10:
> That if thou shalt confess with thy mouth the Lord Jesus, and shalt believe in thine heart that God hath raised him from the dead, thou shalt be saved.
>
> For with the heart man believeth unto righteousness; and with the mouth confession is made unto salvation.

When a man confesses with his mouth Jesus as lord and believes in his heart* that God raised Jesus from the dead, God creates a new spirit in the man, the man who before this confession had just a body and soul.** The moment you

---

*"Heart" is the figure of speech *catachresis* and means "the innermost part of the mind."

**II Peter 2:12 and Jude 10 refer to the men of body and soul as "brute beasts."

33

believe in the depth of your innermost being that God raised Jesus from the dead, you are saved. You have eternal life abiding within.

This is the miracle of conversion, the new birth, a miracle of God whereby a man or woman of body and soul becomes a new creation in Him thus having body, soul, and spirit.

For a man to believe with his heart that God raised Jesus from the dead is "believing unto righteousness." Only after a person believes unto righteousness is it possible to confess Jesus as lord. In this confession lies the salvation that a man receives because he believes.

What does the word "salvation" mean? It means wholeness or soundness: mental, physical, spiritual. Colossians 2:10 defines "wholeness" as "complete." God has made us "completely complete," having all things needed in this life and in that which is to come.

Righteousness, on the other hand, is our God-given ability to stand and walk before God without any sense of sin, guilt, or fear. Righteousness is ours because of believing, and believing only. We do not work for righteousness; for if we did, it would be something we earned. We cannot work for righteousness; we simply accept the righteousness of God as a gift. The *unqualified*

commitment gives both righteousness and wholeness.

> Ephesians 2:8 and 9:
> For by grace are ye saved through faith;
> and that not of yourselves: *it is* the gift of
> God:
>
> Not of works, lest any man should boast.
>
> Ephesians 4:7:
> But unto every one of us is given grace
> according to the measure of the gift of
> Christ.

All born-again believers have "the faith of
Jesus Christ," which is the measure given to
everyone when he believes.* After a person has
confessed with his mouth the Lord Jesus and

---

*Romans 3:22: "Even the righteousness of God *which is*
by faith of Jesus Christ unto all and upon all them that
believe: for there is no difference."

Romans 12:3: "For I say, through the grace given unto
me, to every man that is among you, not to think *of
himself* more highly than he ought to think; but to think
soberly, according as God hath dealt to every man the
measure of faith."

Galatians 2:20: "I am crucified with Christ: neverthe-
less I live; yet not I, but Christ liveth in me: and the life
which I now live in the flesh I live by the faith of the
Son of God, who loved me, and gave himself for me."

has believed in his heart that God raised Jesus from the dead, he is a privileged son of God with access to all His promises. All born-again believers have a legal right and opportunity to receive what God has made available. All have the same righteousness, the same amount of faith, and the same perfection before God.

Do you believe that what God has promised He is able to perform? If you do, you will see mighty signs, miracles, and wonders in your life. You must believe that God is not only *able* but also *willing* to perform what He has promised.

> Ephesians 1:7:
> In whom [Jesus Christ] we have redemption through his blood, the forgiveness of sins, according to the riches of his grace.

We have redemption through his blood according to the riches of His grace. Do you believe God is rich in grace? "For God so loved...that he gave his only begotten Son...." Would you call that rich in grace? I would. Ephesians says that we have received redemption, so we don't need to beg for it. The only thing we must do is receive it.

Colossians 1:13 and 14:
Who hath delivered [past tense] us from the power of darkness, and hath translated [past tense] *us* into the kingdom of [by] his dear Son:

In whom we have redemption through his blood, *even* the forgiveness of sins.

If God has delivered us from the power of darkness (that is, the power of Satan) how can we be under that sinister power any longer? If we have been delivered, why look further for deliverance? Why wait for deliverance when it has already been made available. Satan has no legal rights over a believer because all believers have been delivered from Satan's power through Jesus Christ. What God accomplished for us when He rescued us from the power of Satan we can appropriate to ourselves when we believe. So the next time you get sick, say, "Look here, headache [cold, or whatever negative symptom it may be], you have no power over me. You were defeated over nineteen hundred years ago. It says so in the Word, and I believe the Word; therefore, be gone from me." When we have salvation, we have wholeness, even physical wholeness, if we simply accept it.

We have nothing to stand upon for our completeness except the revealed Word of God. When we stand upon the Word, we have only one way of life, and that is the way of Christ Jesus. In him we have wholeness.

> II Corinthians 5:7:
> (For we walk by faith [believing], not by sight.)

The Bible says that we are to believe first, and then we will see. We stand upon the Word and declare the Word. If I pray for the sick and no one is healed, I continue praying for the sick because the Word says healing is available. If no one believed in receiving the power from the Holy Spirit, I would go right on teaching about the holy spirit because the Bible admonishes in Ephesians 5:18, "...be not drunk with wine, wherein is excess; but be filled with the Spirit." We must walk by believing the promises of God's Word; then the fulfillment of the promise is guaranteed to us even though we may not see the results immediately.

When you belong to Christ, you are a son of God. The moment you become a child of God, you become heir to everything that God has made available.

Romans 8:17:
And if children, then heirs; heirs of God,
and joint-heirs with Christ....

How can you then, as a Christian, talk neg-
atively? How can you continue to be full of
fear? How can you go out in the community
and act like you are defeated? You are not defeated. Satan has been defeated, and the power
of God is in you today.

Romans 8:11:
But if the Spirit of him that raised up Jesus
from the dead dwell in you, he that raised
up Christ from the dead shall also quicken
your mortal bodies by his Spirit that
dwelleth in you.

Do you want your body quickened—made
alive, vital, spry? The Word says that if you
will make the unqualified commitment of confessing Jesus as your savior and lord while
believing that God raised Jesus from the dead,
not only are you made alive spiritually but also
your physical body is made alive even now.

Since you have the spirit from God within,
you are righteous; you are no longer separated

from God. After God gives all this, you then have a responsibility. He says you are to be renewed in your mind.

> Ephesians 4:23 and 24:
> And be renewed in the spirit of your mind;
>
> And that ye put on the new man, which after God is created in righteousness and true holiness.

You are not only to be born again of the spirit from God, but you must change your thinking patterns.

> Philippians 4:8:
> Finally, brethren, whatsoever things are true, whatsoever things *are* honest, whatsoever things *are* just, whatsoever things *are* pure, whatsoever things *are* lovely, whatsoever things *are* of good report; if *there be* any virtue, and if *there be* any praise, think on these things.

Change what you put in your mind. To change the food you are sending to your mind is to "renew your mind." Think those things which are true, honest, just, pure, lovely, and of good report.

If you by your free will accept Christ as your savior and renew your mind according to the Word, you will find that every word I have written to you is true. I challenge you to stand upon the Word of God, declare your authority in Christ, and claim your rights. The Amplified Version translates a verse in Romans so vividly.

Romans 10:11:
The Scripture says, No man who believes in Him [who adheres to, relies on, and trusts in Him] will [ever] be put to shame *or* be disappointed (The Amplified New Testament).

Let us make our *unqualified commitment;* let us confess Jesus as lord and believe that God raised him from the dead. We will never be disappointed.

Chapter Three

HOW TO BE A CHRISTIAN

THE SEARCHER: For years I have tried to be a Christian. I have tried and failed so many times that I am not going to try again because I have no faith left to try.

THE TEACHER: What did you try and in what have you lost faith?

THE SEARCHER: I suppose I tried to get God in my life, but I have been defeated, so I have lost faith in myself. You see, I really wanted to be a Christian, to have God's presence, guidance, and help in life. I took special instructions, I joined the church, I tried hard to be a Christian; but in my heart I knew there was no change. I went to the altar again and again, and yet I received nothing. I have sought and cried after God so much and so many times that I feel that I am a complete failure.

THE TEACHER: Did you ever stop to think that salvation is a gift, that it is unnecessary for you to go anywhere to get it? You can find God anywhere and miss Him everywhere. Do you realize that receiving salvation is not dependent upon what you do but what Christ Jesus did for you? Do you realize that to be a child of God, to receive eternal life, to be saved, converted, born again, is to receive something instead of giving something?

You become a Christian by receiving a gift from the very heart of God directly to you. You, like so many others, thought that receiving Christ depended upon what you gave up, what you surrendered, how much sin you confessed. It doesn't.

You become a Christian by believing that God raised Jesus from the dead, by confessing him as lord in your life.

THE SEARCHER: Surely it can't be as simple as that. I thought and heard and was taught that I must *do* certain things and *give up* other things.

THE TEACHER: If that were true, then you would be earning your salvation; you would be working for it. There is nothing in the Bible that indicates such a process. Look at Isaiah 53:6: "All we like sheep have gone astray; we have turned every one to his own way; and the Lord hath laid on him the iniquity of us all."

God is describing you as well as the rest of us. You have turned to your own way. That is why you are lost. But God laid on Jesus the iniquity of us all. You by your good works and efforts cannot save yourself. God simply laid your sins on Jesus. So far there is no requirement on your part, is there?

Notice John 3:16: "For God so loved the world, that he gave his only begotten Son, that whosoever believeth in him should not perish, but have everlasting life."

This is the Father, God, giving His Son as your substitute and requesting simply that you believe God did this for you and that you claim Jesus as your savior. He does not ask you to do a thing except to *believe,* and believing is acting upon what the Word says He did for you.

No, you have not sinned so much that Jesus cannot save you. Notice His Word in Hebrews 7:25: "Wherefore he is able also to save them to the uttermost that come unto God by him, seeing he ever liveth to make intercession for them."

Jesus saves to the uttermost, and as you notice, there is still no work on your part except believing to receive what he has done.

Romans 10:9 and 10 says, "That if thou shalt confess with thy mouth the Lord Jesus, and shalt believe in thine heart that God hath raised him from the dead, thou shalt be saved. For with the heart man believeth unto righteousness; and with the mouth confession is made unto salvation."

Let us look at these verses closely. If you confess with your mouth Jesus as your lord, you are acting on your believing. You still have not done any works for your salvation, have you? This is not hard to do, is it? Your own way thus far has not been a happy way, a way of joy and peace, nor a successful way. It has been a way of hardship and defeat. Romans 5:1 says, "Therefore being justified by faith, we have peace with God through our Lord Jesus Christ." We are justified in him, and we have peace with God.

Now God says that this is all yours and that He wants you to change from being the lord of your own life by yielding and confessing with your mouth Jesus as your lord.

THE SEARCHER: That's easy for me to do. I know that God sent Jesus into the world and that he was raised from the dead. It's easy to confess Jesus as lord.

THE TEACHER: If you have confessed Jesus as lord, what does the Word say that you are?

THE SEARCHER: That I am saved.

THE TEACHER: Do you believe that God raised Jesus from the dead, and have you confessed Jesus as lord?

THE SEARCHER: I do believe, and I have confessed. But I never thought salvation was that easy to receive. I am a child of God now?

THE TEACHER: I John 3:2: "Beloved, now are we the sons of God, and it doth not yet appear what we shall be: but we know that, when he shall appear...we shall see him as he is."

How do you know you are born again and a child of God?

THE SEARCHER: Because the Word says I am. I believe God raised Jesus from the dead, and I confessed him as my lord, so the Word declares I am a child of God.

But what about having eternal life?

THE TEACHER: I John 5:13: "These things have I written unto you that believe on the name of the Son of God; that ye may know that ye have eternal life, and that ye may believe on the name of the Son of God."

Do you believe on the name of Jesus?

THE SEARCHER: I most assuredly do.

THE TEACHER: Then what have you?

THE SEARCHER: I have eternal life. Now I know according to the Word I do not have to wait until I die to find out whether or not I have eternal life. I have eternal life now.

But what about this righteousness of God that makes it possible for me to stand in His presence without any sense of sin, guilt, and defeat; do I have that too?

THE TEACHER: Notice II Corinthians 5:21: "For he hath made him *to be* sin for us, who knew no sin; that we might be made the righteousness of God in him."

God made Jesus to be sin that you might become the righteousness of God in him. If he became sin for you and you accept him as your savior (your substitute), you are made the righteousness of God in him now.

THE SEARCHER: Have all the gifts of God been given so freely?

THE TEACHER: Ephesians 2:8-10 says, "For by grace are ye saved through faith; and that not of yourselves: *it is* the gift of God: Not of works, lest any man should boast. For we are his workmanship, created in Christ Jesus unto good works, which God hath before ordained that we should walk in them."

THE SEARCHER: I never dreamed that receiving Christ could be as easy as that. I now know that I am a new creature in Christ, having eternal life now, and that I am righteous before God, and Satan has no more power over me if I give him no place. How I thank God through Jesus my new savior and wonderful lord!

Chapter Four

YOUR POWER OF ATTORNEY

Every person in the world wants a good name. People desire to be well-thought-of, and rightly so. I want to have a good name, and I want people to think well of me.

But many people's names today are not respected. A man says to you, "I'll pay you on such and such a day." When that day comes, he does not pay. Someone promises, "I'll meet you at such and such a time." When that time comes, he is not there but has left you waiting. Such a person's name is not respected because he has not put off lying.*

I know that Christ is in me** and I am in him.† No matter what people may say, no matter

---

*Ephesians 4:25: "Wherefore putting away lying, speak every man truth with his neighbour: for we are members one of another."

**Colossians 1:27: "To whom God would make known what *is* the riches of the glory of this mystery among the Gentiles; which is Christ in you, the hope of glory."

†Romans 8:1: "*There is* therefore now no condemnation to them which are in Christ Jesus, who walk not after the flesh, but after the Spirit."

51

what the world may say, my name is written in the Book of Life. But, in order for us to be able to help ourselves and others, we must know more: we must know what power we have.

What is the power of attorney? What is it to have the power of attorney in your life or in the life of the Church? Do you know? The power of attorney is *the legal right to use the name of the person who has given you the power*. This power is limited only to the extent of the resources behind that name. If the Church has been given the power of attorney, it has only as much power as is in the name of Jesus Christ. If the name of Jesus Christ has power, and that name has been given to you, then you have the power of attorney to execute in that name whatever resources he has available.

> Ephesians 1:17:
> That the God of our Lord Jesus Christ, the Father of glory, may give unto you the spirit of wisdom and revelation in the knowledge of him.

The purpose that God had in mind in giving His Son's name to us is set forth in Ephesians.

Ephesians 1:18-23:

The eyes of your understanding being enlightened; that ye may know what is the hope of his calling, and what the riches of the glory of his inheritance in the saints,

And what *is* the exceeding greatness of his power to usward who believe, according to the working of his mighty power,

Which he wrought in Christ, when he raised him from the dead, and set *him* at his own right hand in the heavenly *places,*

Far above all principality, and power, and might, and dominion, and every name that is named, not only in this world, but also in that which is to come:

And hath put all *things* under his feet, and gave him *to be* the head over all *things* to the church,

Which is his body, the fulness of him that filleth all in all.

All the individuals in the true Church (Body of believers) may claim the power in the name of Jesus Christ. But before we study the power we have been given, I want to show you three reasons for the power in his name.

First of all, Jesus *inherited* a more excellent name than any other name in heaven and in earth. He inherited it because he was the only begotten of the Father. This gave him the legal rights of a firstborn son. He is greater than any of the angels or any other individual human being who has lived or who will ever live. In God's presence, next to Jesus Christ stand the believers. Did you know that?

> Romans 8:17:
> And if children, then heirs; heirs of God, and joint-heirs with Christ....

Jesus said, "I came from the Father," and another time he said, "My Father and I are one." "He who has seen me has seen the Father." Remember? Jesus inherited a wonderful name.

Secondly, God *gave* Jesus a name, a name which is above every name.

> Philippians 2:9 and 10:
> Wherefore God also hath highly exalted him, and given him a name which is above every name:
>
> That at the name of Jesus every knee should bow, of *things* in heaven, and *things* in earth, and *things* under the earth.

In the third place, Jesus *acquired* for himself a name above every name.

> Ephesians 4:8:
> Wherefore he saith, When he ascended up on high, he led captivity captive....

> Colossians 2:15:
> *And* having spoiled principalities and powers, he made a shew of them openly, triumphing over them in it.

Jesus achieved these things. He acquired this name by his conquest of sin, by his conquest of the Devil, hell, sickness, and disease. He acquired an exalted name because of his achievements.

The power which Jesus acquired is the legal right of every born-again believer. But for a believer to manifest Christ's power in his life, he must renew his mind according to the Word of God.

> Romans 12:2:
> And be not conformed to this world: but be ye transformed by the renewing of your mind, that ye may prove what *is* that good, and acceptable, and perfect, will of God.

We must make our minds think as the Word dictates so we may prove the will of God.

In order to understand the power in the name of Jesus Christ that is ours, I will take you directly into the Word of God.

> Matthew 1:21:
> And she shall bring forth a son, and thou shalt call his name JESUS: for he shall save his people from their sins.

The prophecy says this child's name shall be Jesus. "Jesus" means "savior."

> Matthew 1:23:
> Behold, a virgin shall be with child, and shall bring forth a son, and they shall call his name Emmanuel, which being interpreted is, God with us.

His name means "he is our savior," and God is with us through him as you can be with me through your children.

> Acts 4:12:
> Neither is there salvation in any other: for there is none other name under heaven given among men, whereby we must be saved.

There is no other name but Jesus Christ whereby we can be saved. We cannot be saved by just belonging to a church or by attending church on Christmas and Easter. We must be saved by confessing the Lord Jesus Christ and by believing that God raised him from the dead.*

> Acts 2:38:
> Then Peter said unto them, Repent, and be baptized every one of you in the name of Jesus Christ for the remission of sins, and ye shall receive the gift of the Holy Ghost.

> John 14:13 and 14:
> And whatsoever ye shall ask in my name [There is that wonderful name again.], that will I do, that the Father may be glorified in the Son.

> If ye shall ask any thing in my name, I will do *it*.

The blessing of using the name of Jesus Christ belongs to us because we belong to the Body

---

*Romans 10:9 and 10: "That if thou shalt confess with thy mouth the Lord Jesus, and shalt believe in thine heart that God hath raised him from the dead, thou shalt be saved. For with the heart man believeth unto righteousness; and with the mouth confession is made unto salvation."

of Christ, the Church. Paul said, "I pray that God may open your understanding so that you will see some of the riches of the inheritance of the saints in the precious name—Jesus."*

In Acts 3 again we note the mighty name of Jesus Christ on the day Peter and John came to the Temple and spoke to the man at the gate who was begging for alms. Did Peter and John go down on their knees and plead with God for an hour to heal the man? No. What does the record say?

> Acts 3:6 and 7:
> Then Peter said, Silver and gold have I none; but such as I have give I thee: In the name of Jesus Christ of Nazareth rise up and walk.
>
> And he took him by the right hand, and lifted *him* up: and immediately his feet and ancle bones received strength.

In the name of Jesus Christ there is power. Acts says that the man stood up and walked as the disciple took him by the hand.

---

*Ephesians 1:18: "The eyes of your understanding being enlightened; that ye may know what is the hope of his calling, and what the riches of the glory of his inheritance in the saints."

Acts 3:16:
And his name through faith in his
name...hath given him this perfect soundness in the presence of you all.

Paul used the mighty name of Jesus as recorded
in Acts 16 to deliver another enslaved person.

Acts 16:16-18:
And it came to pass, as we went to prayer,
a certain damsel possessed with a spirit of
divination met us, which brought her mas-
ters much gain by soothsaying:

The same followed Paul and us, and cried,
saying, These men are the servants of the
most high God, which shew unto us the
way of salvation.

And this did she many days. But Paul, being
grieved, turned and said to the spirit, I command thee in the name of Jesus Christ to
come out of her. And he came out the same
hour.

What power the Church has today in the name
of Jesus Christ! We need to claim that power.
Today's Church has never used the power of his
name to any great extent; and without using it,
the Church can never manifest power. In the

name of Jesus Christ the sick are healed. In the name of Jesus Christ devils are cast out. In the name of Jesus Christ people are freed from mental bondage. What a wonderful privilege and power the Church has.

> Philippians 3:10:
> That I may know him, and the power of his resurrection....

What a joy it is to belong to the Church. When we belong to the Church, we belong to the greatest and most powerful body in the world; there is nothing like the Church anywhere. The Church has such great power that even the gates of hell cannot prevail against it. That is why the Devil cannot harm the people of the Church when they know the name of Jesus Christ and use that name, believing in it. Can you see why our prayers must be answered when we believe that Christ is in us? We can receive anything from God that He has promised in the Word if we only know and believe it. Everything that has been revealed in the Word we can thank God for, and if we believe, it will come to pass.

> Colossians 3:17:
> And whatsoever ye do in word or deed, *do*

all in the name of the Lord Jesus, giving thanks to God and the Father by him.

Ephesians 5:20:
Giving thanks always for all things unto God and the Father in the name of our Lord Jesus Christ.

Do everything in the name of the Lord Jesus, giving thanks always.

Philippians 4:19:
But my God shall supply all your need according to his riches in glory by Christ Jesus.

In other words, all your needs are guaranteed to be supplied by Christ Jesus.

I Corinthians 6:11:
And such were some of you: but ye are washed, but ye are sanctified, but ye are justified in the name of the Lord Jesus, and by the Spirit of our God.

You have been washed and sanctified, and you have been justified in his name; but you must receive it before you will manifest it. Isn't that wonderful! We have all power in that name. We have the power of attorney that when we use the name of Jesus Christ, powerful, positive things must happen.

> Hebrews 13:15:
> By him therefore let us offer the sacrifice of praise to God continually, that is, the fruit of *our* lips giving thanks to his name.

> James 5:14 and 15:
> Is any sick among you? let him call for the elders of the church; and let them pray over him, anointing him with oil in the name of the Lord:

> And the prayer of faith shall save the sick, and the Lord shall raise him up; and if he have committed sins, they shall be forgiven him.

Do elders in the Church have power? Elders have power to move the very gates of hell! The Word says so.

> I John 3:23:
> And this is his commandment, That we should believe on the name of his Son Jesus Christ, and love one another, as he gave us commandment.

We should love one another because of the name of Jesus Christ.

The Church has the power of attorney, the right to use the name of Jesus Christ. I have shown you the scriptural passages teaching of the name of Jesus Christ, showing the power that is behind that name.

Ask yourself honestly, "Do I have the power of attorney?" You do have the right, the God-given authority, to use the name of Jesus Christ and see things come to pass. Yet for years and years people inside the fellowship of believers have seen but few positive results. Why? Just to say the *name of Jesus Christ* is not all that is necessary; you must *believe* that when you are saying it, things will come to pass. All power is energized by believing, and it is up to *you* to operate believing. Believing is action. You must know what the Word of God says and then act upon that Word. As you hear the Word and act upon it, God will answer your requests.

Now that you know you have the power of attorney, use it! What value is it to you to have money in the bank if you do not know you have it? It is the same situation as when we have all the power in the name of Jesus Christ and do not realize it. We have Christ in us, so we have the power of attorney. In the name of Jesus Christ activate that power and live the more abundant life.

Chapter Five

KEY TO POWER

When God created Adam and placed him in the garden of Eden, He gave Adam certain legal rights. These legal rights were not Adam's by nature, not innate rights. These legal rights were conferred rights. Whenever you receive conferred rights, you not only have the privilege and opportunity of having them, but also the possibility of their forfeiture.

God conferred upon Adam the authority and power to rule the earth with all its creatures.* Thus God limited Himself by giving that legal responsibility to Adam. Among other legal rights which God conferred upon Adam were the rights to perfect love, to complete joy, to happiness, to perfect health. The right of everlasting life was another conferred right.

---

*Genesis 1:26: "And God said, Let us make man in our image, after our likeness: and let them have dominion over the fish of the sea, and over the fowl of the air, and over the cattle, and over all the earth, and over every creeping thing that creepeth upon the earth."

Adam—or man in general—not only had certain conferred rights, but he also had natural rights. These natural rights cannot be forfeited. Unlike a natural right, you can use a legal right in whatever way you choose though you do not have the moral right to do so. The legal right to use that which is conferred upon you is absolutely yours. If I conferred upon a person a college degree having certain rights and privileges, the person could take the power that is latent in that degree and use it for good or for evil, use it to benefit man or to harm man.

This truth may be further illustrated by thinking in terms of a court of law. A legal will wherein is stipulated that a certain sum of money has been given to you is read in court. Would you then say that the sum of money is yours? Yes, you would, because it has been legally conferred upon you. After it has been conferred and you receive that sum of money, you may spend it wisely or foolishly, whichever you choose.

Anything which is conferred upon man may be used well or poorly. When God gave Adam all the privileges mentioned in the Word, God also conferred on Adam certain legal rights which in turn gave him absolute control over the privileges granted him. Adam took those legal rights and *transferred* by his own willful decision the authority and power of those rights to Satan. Adam could have refused Eve's enticing offer to sin; however, through freedom of choice, he took his conferred rights, the rulership of the earth, and gave them to Satan. With that decision man lost the legal rights God had given him, forfeiting these rights to another.

The original sin of man had legal consequences. Adam had the right to transfer the authority and the power and the dominion he had because God had conferred it upon him. But Adam committed treason in doing so. Transferring to Satan, God's archenemy, the power which God had originally conferred upon Adam, was treason. Since that day, Romans 8:22 records that "...the whole creation [earth] groaneth and travaileth in pain together [even] until now."

Sin and the consequences of sin were upon man from that day when Satan received the legal right to rule over man and over all the earth. Satan has a legal right now to rule over the unsaved men and over the entire world. Thus when Adam sinned, Satan, who was the supreme enemy of God, obtained absolute control over all that which God had originally given to Adam.

The redemption of man from this fallen state was a most unique act. We must always remember that God is absolutely just. When He makes a legal commitment, He honors it. When God conferred upon Adam certain legal rights and Adam transferred them to Satan, God had to recognize the transferred legal rights.

God, being just, must of necessity redeem man on legal grounds to be just to Himself, to man, and to Satan. In order to accomplish this complete justice, the redeemer had to come to earth. This redeemer had to be a man because it was man who had committed the original sin.

In order to complete all the requirements of justice, the Holy Spirit brought about the conception of Jesus, who was to be the Christ. The child was born of a woman. He was absolute man, but the power of Satan had no authority over him, for there was no death within his body because the life in his blood was sinless or pure and, subsequently, incorruptible.

At various places in the New Testament we read that the blood of Jesus Christ cleanses from all sin.* It could not cleanse had it not been clean.

---

*I John 1:7: "But if we walk in the light, as he is in the light, we have fellowship one with another, and the blood of Jesus Christ his Son cleanseth us from all sin."

The child Jesus was not a subject of death nor a subject of Satan. Satan knew God's purpose, and he tried to frustrate the legal redemption plan by having Herod execute a decree that all children two years and under throughout the entire province were to be killed. Satan knew that if Jesus were to live and grow up, he would reclaim what man had lost and which were now the legal rights of Satan.

Every step that God took through Jesus Christ was a step on legal grounds. Man's redemption is on legal grounds. Jesus met the just demands of God by being human, yet believing perfectly the will of God. He met the demands of a just God for all sinners for all time. Hebrews 4:15 says that the Son of God "was in all points tempted like as *we are, yet* without sin."

Redemption included his crucifixion, as I Peter tells us.

> I Peter 2:24:
> Who his own self bare our sins in his own body on the tree, that we, being dead to sins, should live unto righteousness: by whose stripes ye were healed.

Jesus paid the full legal price for man's sin and the consequences of sin.* He descended into hell (the grave), and sometime between the resurrection and his appearance to Mary, in his resurrected body, he preached to the imprisoned spirits.** He legally broke the chains of authority and power of Satan. Jesus bought back what Adam had legally transferred to Satan. Since the time of Christ's resurrection and the giving of the holy spirit on the day of Pentecost, Satan's power and dominion over man are broken. There is absolutely no control that Satan has or legally holds over any saved man.

Jesus Christ ascended into heaven and took with him the tokens of his victory over the Devil.

> Ephesians 4:8-10:
> Wherefore he saith, When he ascended up on high, he led captivity captive, and gave gifts unto men.
>
> (Now that he ascended, what is it but that he also descended first into the lower parts of the earth?

---

*Hebrews 9:12: "Neither by the blood of goats and calves, but by his own blood he entered in once into the holy place, having obtained eternal redemption *for us*."

**I Peter 3:19: "By which also he went and preached unto the spirits in prison."

He that descended is the same also that ascended up far above all heavens, that he might fill all things.)

On the grounds of Jesus' complete victory, the sinner today has a legal right to salvation. If Jesus Christ had not completed that just victory by being a man and defeating Satan and his power, there would not be a person reading this book who could claim salvation on legal grounds. Christ's completed victory gives the born-again Christian legal rights.

You have a legal right to eternal life because of what Jesus did. You have a legal right to victory over all sin and the consequences of sin. Everything that man lost in Adam, Christ has legally redeemed for mankind. You have a legal right today to a home in heaven. You have a legal right to use the authority of the name of Jesus Christ in prayer in order to get results.* You have a legal right to the Father's protection, care, and guidance. You have a legal right to be a son of God, a friend of God, an heir, yes, a joint heir with Christ Jesus in the family

---

*Philippians 2:10: "That at the name of Jesus every knee should bow, of *things* in heaven, and *things* in earth, and *things* under the earth."

71

of God.* You have a legal right to receive the indwelling presence of the holy spirit. You have a legal right to be changed at the second coming,** if you are alive at that time. You have a legal right to an immortal body.† You have a legal right to an inheritance in the new heaven and the new earth. This is only a portion of the legal rights because of what Jesus Christ did. He bought back and delivered to God the full redemption of man. Jesus Christ purchased you, and his purchase was full and complete. By his purchase we have legal rights which are a gift of grace.

Christians have a delegated authority today which God in Christ has given. But the Church has failed to claim and appropriate its just rights. The Church has not claimed its rights, power, and authority because Satan has talked us out

---

*Romans 8:17: "And if children, then heirs; heirs of God, and joint-heirs with Christ; if so be that we suffer with *him,* that we may be also glorified together."

**I Thessalonians 4:17: "Then we which are alive *and* remain shall be caught up together with them in the clouds, to meet the Lord in the air: and so shall we ever be with the Lord."

†I Corinthians 15:52 and 53: "In a moment, in the twinkling of an eye, at the last trump: for the trumpet shall sound, and the dead shall be raised incorruptible, and we shall be changed. For this corruptible must put on incorruption, and this mortal *must* put on immortality."

of it. My friend the late Rufus Moseley used to say, "God is all the time trying to do the best He can for you, and the Devil is all the time trying to do the worst for you; the way you vote determines the election."

There is only one good power in the world—the power of God. Satan also has power, but only destructive power, which he can use when people permit him to rule them.

Because of our legal rights in Christ Jesus, we do not approach God like a beggar asking for food. We go to God as sons appropriating, by believing, our legal authority and right. When I go to God in prayer, I know the promises of God, and I believe God. God is faithful to His promises, and I claim my legal rights before Him as a son.

The moment a person confesses Jesus Christ as lord in his life, believing in his heart that God raised him from the dead, he becomes a son of God, being born of His Spirit.* If we are sons, we are heirs. According to Romans 8:17

---

*Romans 10:9 and 10: "That if thou shalt confess with thy mouth the Lord Jesus, and shalt believe in thine heart that God hath raised him from the dead, thou shalt be saved. For with the heart man believeth unto righteousness; and with the mouth confession is made unto salvation."

we are joint heirs with Christ. We have a legal right to everything that Christ had, if we will believe. Everything Jesus did while here upon earth we may do, and more, if we believe.* This is a gift of God's grace.

God will do what He said He would do. We have believed so many things which Satan has said, but we have believed so little of what God has said. How often God makes a promise in the Word saying He will do so-and-so, but we do not believe a word of it. A friend makes us a promise, and we believe every word; but when God gives us promises in the Bible, we say, "Oh, no, that cannot be true. That was all right for the spiritual men like the apostles, but not for Christians like me." Chapter and verse please to back up such a statement!

Christ has delegated his authority to the believers who make up the Church, the saints of the household of faith. If the Church fails to assume its responsibility and its delegated opportunities, God's power and authority are paralyzed. God has moved in Jesus Christ. Jesus Christ moved

---

*John 14:12: "Verily, verily, I say unto you, He that believeth on me, the works that I do shall he do also; and greater *works* than these shall he do; because I go unto my Father."

to regain legal rights for man. Now it is man's move in the authority and power delegated to him by Jesus Christ, for Satan has no legal rights over the converted, born-again man.

> Romans 6:14:
> For sin shall not have dominion over you ....

Satan, however, still has definite legal rights over the sinner. The unconverted sinner legally belongs in body and soul to the Devil. But Christ has broken that power for us who are born of God's Spirit and know His power within us.

Note Christ's authority and power.

> Philippians 2:5-11:
> Let this mind be in you, which was also in Christ Jesus:
>
> Who, being in the form of God, thought it not robbery to be equal with God:
>
> But made himself of no reputation, and took upon him the form of a servant, and was made in the likeness of men:
>
> And being found in fashion as a man, he humbled himself, and became obedient unto death, even the death of the cross.

Wherefore God also hath highly exalted him, and given him a name which is above every name:

That at the name of Jesus every knee should bow, of *things* in heaven, and *things* in earth, and *things* under the earth;

And *that* every tongue should confess that Jesus Christ *is* Lord, to the glory of God the Father.

I Corinthians 3:21 and 23:

...For all things are yours.

And ye are Christ's; and Christ *is* God's.

If I Corinthians 3:21 and 23 are true, then rise up like men of God and claim your believer's delegated authority! The power and authority of Christ is delegated to us through the name of Jesus Christ. It is his wonderful, matchless, powerful name, when named from our heart and on our lips, that cancels the forces of evil. We have a delivering Christ, and his authority is our authority to act in his name through the Church he established.

The words in Mark are true for every believer.

> Mark 16:17-20:
> And these signs shall follow them that believe; In my name shall they cast out devils; they shall speak with new tongues;
>
> They shall take up serpents; and if they drink any deadly thing, it shall not hurt them; they shall lay hands on the sick, and they shall recover.
>
> So then after the Lord had spoken unto them, he was received up into heaven, and sat on the right hand of God.
>
> And they went forth, and preached every where, the Lord working with *them,* and confirming the word with signs following. Amen.

A believer's delegated authority is the legal right of deliverance from all the powers of the enemy. If you have one thousand dollars in the bank, you have the legal right or authority to write a check for one thousand dollars. It does not take faith to do so. It takes action and boldness.

Unless we claim with action and boldness our delegated rights, we are tying God's hands. God is limited to the extent of a man's believing and obedience. May I urge you to study God's Word diligently so you will know what are your legal rights in Christ Jesus. This is *the key to power.*

Chapter Six

FELLOWSHIP IS THE SECRET

The principal key in a successful Christian life is fellowship with the heavenly Father. Christians manifest the more abundant life in direct proportion to the fellowship they keep with Him. But before a person can have fellowship, he must have sonship. We cannot have fellowship with the Father until we have become His sons. Sonship makes us righteous before God and starts us out in perfect fellowship with our Father; but sustained fellowship depends upon the renewing of our minds according to His Word.*

What happens when a person becomes a child of God and is born into the family of God? At the time of rebirth, the believer is made absolutely and completely righteous—as righteous

---

*A believer has both standing and state in the household of God. His standing remains constant—he always stands as a son. But the state of this believer varies directly with his behavior, that is, his living in fellowship according to the Word.

as Jesus Christ himself. Our righteousness is the righteousness of God. This is given to us by the Father Himself.

> II Corinthians 5:21:
> For he [God] hath made him [Jesus] *to be* sin for us, who knew no sin; that we might be made the righteousness of God in him.

As believers, we have the righteousness of God. This is too marvelous to comprehend. Our standing as sons of the Father means that we are clothed in the righteousness with which Christ Jesus clothed us, not of our works lest any man should boast, but of God's grace and by divine favor.

Oh, that we might believe and see! So many Christians maintain that they have to wait until they die to find out if they have made heaven. The Word says that there is no waiting. Believers are righteous now. They will not come into judgment or condemnation.

> John 5:24:
> Verily, verily, I say unto you, He that heareth my word, and believeth [hearing is not enough, it must be accompanied with believing or corresponding action] on him that

sent me [the Father], hath [already has] everlasting life, and shall not come into condemnation; but is passed from death unto life.

This verse tells us what happens to believers *now*—not what happens when we die. We have everlasting life now.

I was called to the hospital a while ago to see a man supposedly dying of heart trouble. He was in an oxygen tent with his life rapidly waning. The man was unsaved; but God is so great in His mercy and grace that even the unsaved are healed. I ministered to him in the name of Jesus Christ for his physical deliverance. The next day this man said, "If God is so good to heal me, when I have done nothing but live against His will and for the Devil's glory, I want that God." He accepted Jesus Christ as his personal lord and savior. The moment he confessed with his mouth the Lord Jesus and believed in his heart that God raised Jesus from the dead, that moment this man was saved and received eternal life. God gave him righteousness, which is remission of all sin, thus placing the delivered man in the "family of God" and in fellowship with Himself.

> Romans 8:1:
> *There is* therefore now no condemnation to them which are in Christ Jesus....

God, through Christ, has made us legal heirs with Jesus Christ and sets us in perfect fellowship. Job 33:26 says, "...He restoreth unto man his righteousness" (literal translation). Thus a child of God at the time of rebirth is restored in the Father's presence with the Father's own righteousness. In the family of God every believer has the legal standing of a son. To say, as sons, that we are unworthy or unfit or to not forgive ourselves when God has forgiven us, to constantly confess our weakness and inability, to deny our perfect righteousness in Him, is to deny God, His Word, and His power. Many believers are denying what they received when they believed, and thus are critically limiting the ability of God in themselves. This is one of the major tricks Satan tries to work in every believer.

The believer is righteous according to the Word of God, but the believer must, as I John 1:7 says, "...walk in the light, as he [God] is in the light..." to maintain the fellowship, not the relationship, of a son. The believer must walk in the light, walk as God leads, bring his body and soul into subjection to the Word by way of renewing his mind. Renewing the mind to the Word and thereby living as God's Word says we should keeps us in fellowship. Our sonship cannot be challenged because it is dependent upon God and His finished work in Christ Jesus. But our fellowship depends upon our walk before God.

Fellowship with God as our Father *is the secret* to spiritual happiness and power in our day-by-day walk on earth. Without fellowship we cannot bring forth the fruits of the righteousness which we received from God. Fellowship makes the family life a happy one. Broken fellowship does not break the family relationship, but it takes the happiness out of the relationship. If your son disobeys you, he is still your son; it is the fellowship between the two of you which has been injured.

Fellowship is the one thing that makes for a happy situation both in a human and in a spiritual family. Fellowship with God by way of the renewed mind is the key to power; it is the only way to manifest the more abundant life or to manifest that we are "more than conquerors." The mind, renewed according to the Word, may stay in fellowship with God and express the results of the union. John 15:5 says, "I am the vine, ye *are* the branches: He that abideth in me [renews his mind according to the Word]... bringeth forth much fruit...." Not renewing the mind, which is not living as the Word directs, is broken fellowship. Broken fellowship does not break the family relationship between God and His son, but it clouds and mars the relationship, robbing it of its blessings and powers.

When a son is out of fellowship with God, he is not able to get prayers answered. God is not unwilling to answer His son's request, but the broken fellowship on the part of the son leaves his confidence in God shaky and uncertain.

> I John 3:21 and 22:
> Beloved, if our heart condemn us not, *then* have we confidence toward God.
>
> And whatsoever we ask, we receive of him....

Whenever and wherever sons fail to get prayers answered, the cause is broken fellowship, either from not knowing or not living the Word. God is faithful Who has promised, and He will bring it to pass; thus, if it does not come to pass, it is due to a flaw on the man's part.

A radio-design engineer employed by one of the larger manufacturers of radios told me about his most recent experience in believing God. He had designed a new radio and had given instructions for its production when one of the prominent men of the company came to him saying, "You certainly don't know much about designing radios if you think that new design will work in production." This upset my friend and for seven days he was negative and resentful, and the production of the new design was at a standstill. Finally, he came to himself and said, "If God is for me, who can be against me?" So, he talked to Father, saying, "God, You helped me to design this radio, You gave me the desire and the thoughts; therefore, I also now surrender the production to You. I relinquish my hurt feelings regarding it, and I am sorry I have been so negative." Within two days the newly designed radio was in production. The result was amazing. The usual number of rejects in the first fifteen hundred radios is 5 percent or more; however, this particular production had fewer than 4 percent on the first fifteen hundred radios and less than 2 percent by the time production had reached three thousand.

When a son of God is out of fellowship with his heavenly Father, nothing will work; but when fellowship is restored, things begin to operate.

85

Broken fellowship takes the zest out of Christian living. When a son is in fellowship with his earthly father, he will enjoy rights and privileges; but when he is out of fellowship, he will be miserable and defeated. Likewise, a son of God out of fellowship will be miserable and defeated.

We must maintain fellowship if we want the power of God manifested in our day-by-day living. The more abundant life—our deliverance from the power of Satan in this world—depends upon keeping the established fellowship with God.

The Epistle of I John dramatizes a son's relationship and fellowship with God: How to maintain fellowship and what to do when fellowship is broken and needs to be reestablished.

> I John 1:3—2:2:
> ...and truly our fellowship *is* with the Father, and with his Son Jesus Christ.
>
> And these things write we unto you, that your joy may be full. [Fullness of joy in a Christian's life depends upon keeping the fellowship with God unimpaired.]
>
> This then is the message which we have heard of him, and declare unto you, that

God is light, and in him is no darkness at all.

If we say that we have fellowship with him, and walk in darkness [out of fellowship is walking in darkness], we lie, and do not the truth:

But if we walk in the light, as he is in the light, we have fellowship one with another [because we as believers are in Christ], and the blood of Jesus Christ his Son cleanseth us from all sin [wherever we are out of fellowship].

If we say that we have no sin [no broken fellowship], we deceive ourselves, and the truth is not in us [in our minds].

If we confess our sins [broken fellowship], he is faithful and just to forgive us *our* sins [broken fellowship], and to cleanse us from all unrighteousness [every sin is unrighteous].

If we say that we have not sinned [broken fellowship], we make him a liar, and his word is not in us [in our minds].

My little children, these things write I unto you, that ye sin not [it is God's will that we do not get out of fellowship]. And if any man sin [breaks the fellowship], we have an advocate with the Father, Jesus Christ the righteous:

And he is the propitiation for our sins [broken fellowship]: and not for ours only, but also for *the sins* [broken fellowship] *of* the whole world.

God's will for every believer is set forth in I John 2:6 where it is written, "He that saith he abideth in him [God by Christ Jesus] ought himself also so to walk, even as he [Jesus Christ] walked."

The deeper we get into the Word and the deeper the Word gets into us, the richer and fuller becomes our fellowship. To walk in fellowship is to walk in love, for "God is love." Fellowship is *our* continued *relationship with God.* Sonship is *God's* permanent *relationship with us.* Fellowship is maintained only by renewing the mind according to His Word. According to Romans 12:2, "...be ye transformed by the renewing of your mind...." Philippians 2:5 says, "Let this mind be in you, which was also in Christ Jesus." Also Colossians 3:16, "Let the word of Christ dwell in you richly...."

To the extent that the Word richly dwells in us, we have fellowship with God. To the extent that we believe and act according to God's Word, our lives will be full, rich, and fruitful because our fellowship with God is strong. We then have confidence toward God. When we know and live His Word, we are doing His will.

Chapter Seven

WHAT IS TRUE WORSHIP?

I am sure that you have asked yourself many, many times as you've observed different religious groups, different churches, different denominations, just what is worship? Some churches have altars; they have candles, incense, holy water. Other denominations have no symbols at all. You have certainly noticed so many variations that you have thought many times, "If that's the way they worship, why does another group worship so differently?" Each group may have a kernel of truth, but such diversity of religious ritual among Christian believers cannot all be in alignment with the Word.

What is true worship? The verses that are critically important to understand are spoken by Jesus in John 4.

> John 4:22-24:
> Ye worship ye know not what: we know what we worship: for salvation is of the Jews [Judeans].

> But the hour cometh, and now is, when the true worshippers shall worship the Father in spirit and in truth: for the Father seeketh such to worship him.

> God *is* a Spirit: and they that worship him must worship *him* in spirit and in truth.

Jesus said, "Ye worship ye know not what...." I believe that is true for most people. Everybody worships. The question is: Are we worshiping rightly? Do we know what, how, or why we worship?

Jesus said about worship that "the hour cometh...when the true worshippers shall worship the Father in spirit [The word "in" is the same Greek word translated "by," "by spirit."] and in truth." Worship the Father how? You shall worship Him not by candles, not by altars, not by Bible reading, not by singing, *but by the spirit*. "In spirit and in truth" is the figure of speech *hendiadys:* two nouns used but one thing meant. "Spirit" is a noun and "truth" is a noun, the double noun being used to doubly emphasize that it is spiritually true, or truly spiritual. The Father seeketh a true worshiper to worship thus—in spirit and in truth. If we can find out what it is to worship God by the spirit, we know how to truly worship.

The question is not what anybody thinks, but what does the Word say? There have been so many ideas brought to Christianity that it is often difficult for even Biblical scholars to distinguish between that which is genuine and that which is counterfeit. In other words, it is hard to separate that which is truly Christianity from that which is religion. Religion is what man has introduced. There is much religion in so-called Christianity, but Christianity does not literally have one ounce of religion in it. Unless you know the difference between religion and Christianity, you will become very confused. Christianity, in a nutshell, is what God wrought in Christ. Christianity is Christ in you, the hope of glory.

The Bible teaches that God is Spirit and that we are to worship Him in spirit and in truth. Jesus told this truth when he spoke to the Samaritan woman. In John 4:20 the woman said to Jesus, "Our fathers worshipped in this mountain; and ye say, that in Jerusalem is the place where men ought to worship." Jesus replied in verse 21, "Woman, believe me, the hour cometh, when ye shall neither in this mountain, nor yet at Jerusalem, worship the Father." How then shall He be worshiped?

Philippians 3:3:
For we are the circumcision, which worship
God in the spirit, and rejoice in Christ Jesus,
and have no confidence in the flesh.

This is true worship. The called of God are
those who "worship God in the spirit, and rejoice
in Christ Jesus."

We rejoice in Christ Jesus, not in Jesus Christ.
There is a great difference. We do not rejoice
in the humiliated one, Jesus, but in the glorified
Christ. Our rejoicing, our worshiping is in the
resurrected Christ. Our rejoicing is not in that
Jesus who was spit on or slapped or persecuted
or derided. We rejoice that he was more than a
conqueror, that he overcame and ascended up
into heaven, that he is seated at the right hand
of God, and that on the day of Pentecost he sent
"forth this, which ye now see and hear," as stated
in Acts 2:33. Rejoice about Christ Jesus, the
humiliated one who has been resurrected and has
ascended into glory.

To worship is to rejoice in Christ Jesus for
what he did, not what we do because the flesh
is weak. Do not judge men by the flesh. Have
no confidence, trust, reliance, nor believing in
the flesh. The flesh is so weak that John 6:63

says, "...the flesh profiteth nothing...." When we have confidence in the flesh, we may assess one man to be better than another on the basis of appearance. Yet, if men are born again of God's Spirit, whose children are they? God's! In God's sight they are equally precious.

There are many things going on under the guise of Christianity which are nothing more than having "confidence in the flesh." But we truly have our confidence in what God wrought in Christ Jesus. Christ Jesus made us presentable to worship God.

> Colossians 1:12:
> Giving thanks unto the Father, which hath made us meet [adequate] to be partakers [to share fully] of the inheritance of the saints in light.

Matthew 15 gives an account of worship, but again it is not true worship.

> Matthew 15:6-9:
> ...Thus have ye made the commandment of God of none effect by your tradition.
>
> *Ye* hypocrites, well did Esaias prophesy of you, saying,

> This people draweth nigh unto me with their mouth, and honoureth me with *their* lips; but their heart is far from me.
>
> But in vain they do worship me, teaching *for* doctrines the commandments of men.

Did their worship look genuine? Did they go through religious ritual? Judging by the flesh, we would have given them the stamp of approval. But what did the Lord say? "In vain they do worship me." Why did they worship in vain? Because they were "teaching *for* doctrines the commandments of men."

Another example of vain worship is recorded in Mark.

> Mark 7:5-9:
> Then the Pharisees and scribes asked him, Why walk not thy disciples according to the tradition of the elders, but eat bread with unwashen hands?
>
> He answered and said unto them, Well hath Esaias prophesied of you hypocrites, as it is written, This people honoureth me with *their* lips, but their heart is far from me.
>
> Howbeit in vain do they worship me, teaching *for* doctrines the commandments of men.

For laying aside the commandment of God, ye hold the tradition of men, *as* the washing of pots and cups: and many other such like things ye do.

And he said unto them, Full well [with full knowledge] ye reject the commandment of God, that ye may keep your own tradition.

What kind of worship is this? Vain worship. Simply performing the traditions of men, a hollow act.

Romans 1:25:
Who [people] changed the truth of God into a lie, and worshipped and served the creature more than the Creator....

They worshiped man more than they worshiped God. Vain worship has been going on for a long time. The children of Israel wandered from God and worshiped in vain. In Acts 7 and Revelation 9 the children of Israel rejecting the preaching of their man of God, Moses, and worshiping devil spirits is recorded.

Acts 7:40-47:
Saying unto Aaron [the children of Israel said to Aaron], Make us gods to go before

us: for *as for* this Moses, which brought us out of the land of Egypt, we wot [know] not what is become of him.

And they made a calf in those days, and offered sacrifice unto the idol, and rejoiced in the works of their own hands.

Then God turned, and gave them up to worship the host of heaven [devil spirits]; as it is written in the book of the prophets, O ye house of Israel, have ye offered to me slain beasts and sacrifices *by the space of* forty years in the wilderness?

Yea, ye took up the tabernacle of Moloch, and the star of your god Remphan, figures which ye made to worship them....

Our fathers had the tabernacle of witness in the wilderness, as he had appointed, speaking unto Moses, that he should make it according to the fashion that he had seen.

Which also our fathers that came after brought in with Jesus [Joshua] into the possession of the Gentiles, whom God drave out before the face of our fathers, unto the days of David;

Who found favour before God, and desired to find a tabernacle for the God of Jacob.

But Solomon built him an house.

Revelation 9:20:

And the rest of the men which were not killed by these plagues yet repented not of the works of their hands, that they should not worship devils, and idols of gold, and silver, and brass, and stone, and of wood: which neither can see, nor hear, nor walk.

Worshiping the Devil and devil spirits and everything related to them is worshiping in vain. Satan tried cajoling even Jesus himself into worshiping in vain.

Matthew 4:8 and 9:

Again, the devil taketh him [Jesus] up into an exceeding high mountain, and sheweth him all the kingdoms of the world, and the glory of them;

And saith unto him, All these things will I give thee, if thou wilt fall down and worship me.

The greatest victory for the Devil would have been to have Jesus worship him. As human beings, we have two, and only two, alternatives of worship—the true God and the Devil. If we worship the true God in spirit, we rejoice in Christ Jesus; we have no confidence in the flesh.

If things surrounding us look black and society seems worse and worse, do not get excited, but stand on the promises of God and worship God in spirit and in truth. No good end can come to those who worship anything but the true God.

> Revelation 19:20:
> And the beast was taken, and with him the false prophet that wrought miracles before him, with which he deceived them that had received the mark of the beast, and them that worshipped his image. These both were cast alive into a lake of fire burning with brimstone.

This destruction can easily be avoided; we must worship God.

> Revelation 22:9:
> Then saith he unto me, See *thou do it* not: for I am thy fellowservant, and of thy brethren the prophets, and of them which keep the sayings of this book: worship God.

How are we going to worship God by the spirit if we are not born again of God's Spirit? It is impossible. If we are born again of God's Spirit, filled with the power of the holy spirit, we can worship the true God by the spirit. And to worship by the spirit we must operate a manifestation of the holy spirit. The manifestation of the spirit which produces true worship is speaking in tongues.

When we worship God by way of speaking in tongues, it is "speaking unto God."

> I Corinthians 14:2:
> For he that speaketh in an *unknown* tongue speaketh not unto men, but unto God....

Speaking in tongues is speaking the "wonderful works of God."

> Acts 2:11:
> Cretes and Arabians, we do hear them speak in our tongues the wonderful works of God.

Speaking in tongues is "magnifying God."

> Acts 10:46:
> For they heard them speak with tongues, and magnify God....

Speaking in tongues is praying perfectly.

> Romans 8:26:
> Likewise the Spirit also helpeth our infir-
> mities: for we know not what we should
> pray for as we ought: but the Spirit itself
> maketh intercession for us....

Speaking in tongues is giving thanks well.

> I Corinthians 14:17:
> For thou verily givest thanks well....

Speaking in tongues is worshiping "in [by] spirit and in truth." Speaking in tongues is true worship. God Who is Spirit is communicating to His gift of holy spirit which is His new creation in me. In other words, God's Spirit speaking to my spirit as evidenced by speaking in tongues is truly worship. How beautiful and yet how misunderstood worship has become.

Chapter Eight

THE BELIEVER'S RESPONSIBILITY

Believers during all eras of history have had the opportunity and responsibility of witnessing to the Word of God. We of the Church Age have our specific "assignment" too. In Philippians 2 the Apostle Paul reveals to us what the condition of the world is and what our responsibilities toward it are.

> Philippians 2:15 and 16:
> That ye may be blameless and harmless, the sons of God, without rebuke, in the midst of a crooked and perverse nation, among whom ye shine as lights in the world;
>
> Holding forth the word of life....

This passage is addressed to the Church. Believers are able to live blameless and harmless lives because they are the sons of God.

What circumstances does God say surround His sons? They live "in the midst of a crooked and perverse nation." As believers, we are right in the middle, set like a hub, with every opportunity to shine as lights in a contorted and distorted world.

In order to shine as lights, we must first know the light which is found in Christ and in the knowledge of God's Word.

> John 12:46:
> I am come a light into the world, that whosoever believeth on me should not abide in darkness.

Christ was that light, but now we are as shining lights holding the Word of God forth as it is in truth the Word of Life. You need not ask a person if he is saved. The Word says to simply hold forth the Word of Life that they may see. The Word is in itself the witness.

Think of the privilege that is ours even to reach one person in a lifetime with the gospel of Light. The person we reach may be a key person in a community or in a whole area. The person you reach for Christ may be the one person who will in turn win hundreds of thousands.

Someone once witnessed to and won the great religious saints of all times; yes, someone who was holding forth the Word of Life. It is a believer's opportunity and responsibility to hold forth the Word in a crooked and perverse world.

In order to effectively hold forth the Word of Life, we as believers must first know and then practice the knowledge told in II Corinthians 5.

> II Corinthians 5:17:
> Therefore if any man *be* in Christ, *he is* a new creature: old things are passed away; behold, all things are become new.

I was taught to believe this scripture meant that when Christ came within a man then that person was a new creature. This is *not* at all what verse 17 of II Corinthians 5 says. Read it again. "Therefore if any man *be* in Christ [in Christ].... " This verse does not say anything about Christ being *in* a man, as does Colossians 1:27: "...Christ in you [in you], the hope of glory."

The miracle of the new birth means *Christ in you*. However, Christ in you does not automatically put him in your mind, *you in Christ*, you in fellowship. Romans 12:2 states that we ourselves have to put on Christ and God's Word in our minds: "...be ye transformed by the renewing of your mind...." Philippians 2:5 stipulates, "Let this mind be in you, which was also in Christ Jesus."

II Corinthians 5:17 is speaking about the believer who has renewed his mind, who has been transformed by the renewing of his mind according to the Christ who lives within. "Therefore if any man *be* in Christ, *he is* a new creature...." It is one thing for Christ to abide *in you;* it is quite another thing for you to abide *in Christ.* When you are in Christ, when you have put Christ in your mind, *then* you have power in manifestation.

> John 15:7:
> If ye abide in me, and my words abide in you, ye shall ask what ye will, and it shall be done unto you.

You become a new creature as you renew your mind according to the Word. "...Old things [in the mind] are passed away...." Old desires, old longings, and old temptations disappear. "...Behold, all things are become new."

II Corinthians 5, after telling us as believers to renew our minds, tells first of our being reconciled to God and then of our responsibility to witness to all men.

> II Corinthians 5:17 and 18:
> Therefore if any man *be* in Christ, *he is* a new creature: old things are passed away; behold, all things are become new.
>
> And all things [when we have renewed our minds, when we are in Christ] *are* of God, who hath reconciled us to himself by Jesus Christ, and hath given to us the ministry of reconciliation.

We are reconciled to God by Jesus Christ. We lost our spiritual connection with God by way of Adam. Because of Adam's disobedience, sin passed on to all men, for all are dead in trespasses and sin. But Jesus came and repaired the broken line; Jesus made the proper connection again. "...All things *are* of God, who hath reconciled us to himself by Jesus Christ, and hath given to us the ministry of reconciliation."

Once we are reconciled to God by Jesus Christ, then God gives to us the ministry of reconciliation. Then our job as believers is to reconcile.

What does the word "reconcile" mean? It means to bring back together that which has been separated. God has given to you as a believer that ministry of bringing back to Him those people who are removed. Our responsibility is to tell of the great opportunities every man has in Christ Jesus. We are to simply show forth the love of God, show people that Jesus Christ died for them and was resurrected over nineteen hundred years ago. We must demonstrate the power of God, manifest what a believer has in Christ, show how great Christ is. That is the ministry of reconciliation. What a ministry we have!

> II Corinthians 5:19:
> To wit, that God was in Christ, reconciling the world unto himself, not imputing their trespasses unto them; and hath committed unto us the word of reconciliation.

When Christ abides in your heart, you have the ministry of taking the Word and reconciling people to God.

Isaiah tells of the dire need of people to be brought back to God.

Isaiah 53:6:

All we like sheep have gone astray; we have turned every one to his own way; and the Lord hath laid on him the iniquity of us all.

"All we like sheep have gone astray...." Everyone at one time is lost. Reason: "We have turned every one to his own way." We lost *the* way because we have turned to *our* own way. God had to do something about the dilemma into which we got ourselves, so He reconciled us to Himself through Christ Jesus. How? By laying "on him [Jesus] the iniquity of us all." God laid all our sins and all the sins of every other person on Jesus. The believer's great responsibility is the ministry of reconciliation— putting back together that which has been broken or separated—between God and man. We are to hold forth the Word of Life to all, for all have gone astray. We have already been reconciled to God; now it is our responsibility to hold forth His Word "in the midst of a crooked and perverse nation." When we hold forth the Word of Life, we shine as lights in the world. This is our ministry of reconciliation. This is our responsibility.

PART III

A Christian's
Power Base

PART III

A CHRISTIAN'S POWER BASE

In a previous chapter entitled "What Is True Worship?" we studied briefly what Part III, "A Christian's Power Base," looks at with more detail. With a power base we as Christians don't have to settle for life's "potluck"; we can appropriate the desires of our hearts by exercising the potential power which God has given.

But before we can outwardly manifest that power, we have to activate it. And the key to transforming our potential power into active power lies in our worship, specifically in our speaking in tongues.

The first chapter in this part explains and shows us from the Bible what speaking in tongues is. Then the explanation is followed by the do-it-yourself chapter, "How to Speak in Tongues." A full understanding of the power of speaking in tongues comes in the tremendous study of "Filled to Overflowing." That chapter is a Biblical study of two Greek words—*plēroō* and *plēthō*. The Word of God in a thrilling way tells us that we are not only filled to the brim with the power of God, but we are filled to

113

overflowing. Now is the time to tap in to this power, strength, and abundance which can over-flow into every facet of our lives.

Chapter Nine

SPEAKING IN TONGUES

No one can go any further than he himself has been taught, and a teacher can teach no more than he knows. If you want to help someone else, first you yourself must be helped; otherwise, the blind lead the blind, and they both stumble around. One of the darkest spots of understanding in the Bible concerns the Holy Spirit, both the Giver and the gift of holy spirit. Let us no longer be blind. Let us study God's Word to understand His will.

First of all let us clarify that God is Holy Spirit. When a person is born again, God gives to His new son a gift. And since God is Holy Spirit, He can only give what He is—holy spirit. To help distinguish between God the Giver and His gift: the Giver, Holy Spirit, is always capitalized, while His gift, holy spirit, is not.

A person receives the holy spirit when he confesses Jesus as lord and believes that God raised Jesus from the dead, as Romans 10:9 and 10 directs. The gift of holy spirit has nine parts or manifestations. I Corinthians 12 lists these manifestations: (1) word of wisdom, (2) word of knowledge, (3) faith (believing), (4) gifts of healing, (5) miracles, (6) prophecy, (7) discerning of spirits, (8) tongues, and (9) interpretation of tongues. In this study we want to specifically look at the manifestation of speaking in tongues—*when* one speaks in tongues and *why* one speaks in tongues.

A believer operating the manifestation of the spirit called tongues will be edified spiritually, spiritually built-up. He can operate this manifestation in two situations: in public and in private. (1) The bulk of a believer's speaking in tongues is in his own private life. As such, speaking in tongues in private will be prayer or praise to the Father and, therefore, is *never* interpreted. This prayer and praise is spoken of as "praying in the spirit." (2) A believer can speak in tongues publicly in a believers' meeting. When a person publicly speaks in tongues, he must always interpret. A public message is never a prayer, however; it is a communication from God meant for the people present. Both public and private speaking in tongues are called speaking to God.

When you pray silently in the spirit, you are speaking in tongues. When you speak aloud in a believers' meeting, you are also speaking in tongues. These different usages of speaking in tongues must be kept distinct from each other. We must learn how to operate speaking in tongues, and bring it forth accurately from the Word.

Let us consider speaking in tongues inside the Church. The "Church" in the Word of God refers to the born-again sons of God, filled with the power from the Holy Spirit and operating the manifestations of the spirit. In the Church speaking in tongues *with* interpretation by a believer is a message from God or for God to the body of believers to edify the group of people by way of exhortation and comfort. "To exhort" means "to encourage to a more worthy endeavor." "To comfort" is "to give a quiet serenity, a peacefulness and an acquiescence to the greatness of the things God has to say." Speaking in tongues with its interpretation edifies the Church by encouraging them and/or by comforting them.

This edification, this building up of the body of believers by means of speaking in tongues with interpretation, is a direct message from God as if God Himself is in the believers' meeting. God is speaking to His people. As we speak in tongues and interpret in a believers' meeting

117

today, we receive God's message to that particular gathering. What He wants for us tomorrow, we will find out tomorrow. We do not know now what the specific message is for the future, but we do know what the message is for this particular day if we have ears to hear.

Speaking in tongues privately and speaking in tongues plus interpreting publicly have two distinctly different ways of edifying. The *private message* is a prayer which edifies the *spirit* of the speaker. The *public message* is a communication which edifies the *minds* of the people present, including the speaker. Now, is a person who speaks in tongues and interprets in a believers' meeting edified in his spirit? No. The speaking in tongues in a believers' meeting by one who also interprets does not edify that believer in the spirit, for the spoken message is from God to the people, and the interpretation, in the language of the body of people present, is for the edification of the body of believers. A public message with its interpretation does not nourish the spirit of the speaker but rather edifies the minds of the congregated people.

The Word of God explicitly teaches that when a person speaks in tongues in a believers' meeting, he must interpret to edify the minds of the

Body. However, there are children of God who speak in tongues in a believers' meeting, but their believing or their knowledge is not sufficient to inspire them to interpret. They are what I call "unbelieving believers." They know that they can speak in tongues in their private life and some even speak in believers' meetings, but they do not believe to interpret.

If these "unbelieving believers," who do not believe to interpret, spoke in tongues in the Church, their spirit would be edified under such circumstances. Their speaking would not be a message from God to the people, because if it were, it would have to be interpreted.

To understand this, you must understand the foreknowledge of God. Does God know before I speak in tongues in a believers' meeting whether or not I am going to interpret? God, knowing that I am going to interpret when I speak in tongues, gives a message to the people. Vice versa, God, knowing that I am going to speak in tongues but not interpret, inspires a prayer, again, to edify the speaker's spirit.

In the body of believers, speaking in tongues with interpretation is always a message from God or for God to the people, and its interpretation will edify, build up, the body of believers in their renewed mind by way of exhortation and comfort. Not only are the minds of the believers encouraged and comforted, but I Corinthians 14:22 tells that the given message is a sign to the unbeliever as well. These unbelievers are not the unsaved unbelievers, but rather the unbelieving believers. The word "unbeliever" is a form of *apistia*.* The unbelieving believer needs this sign of hearing someone speak in tongues to know that there is power in believers, that believers do speak in tongues, and that believers do interpret.

Praying privately to God in the spirit or giving a message in tongues with interpretation in a believers' meeting are both called speaking in tongues. The reason for confusion of the two usages is that people are looking for a way to break God's Word. Why don't we look for a way to build the Word rather than to tear it to pieces? We should believe in the integrity of the Word and let the Word speak. Then we harmonize our lives and our believing with the record in the Word. We search the Word to see how the whole Word fits together precisely.

Apistia—the unbelief of one who has had some instruction and teaching but not fully enough to believe.

Apeitheia—the unbelief of one who has been fully instructed and taught but refuses to believe.

In the Church, speaking in tongues must be done by believers who believe to interpret, or it is not being used for the designed purpose which God intended. Those Christians who speak in tongues but who do not believe to interpret in a believers' meeting are simply speaking a prayer. These people are *not* to speak aloud in the Church but are to pray silently in tongues to themselves and to God.

> I Corinthians 14:2:
> For he that speaketh in an *unknown* tongue speaketh not unto men, but unto God: for no man understandeth *him;* howbeit in the spirit he speaketh mysteries.

The speaking is an unknown tongue to the speaker. The word "unknown" is in italics and need not be there at all, as it is redundant. "Tongues," by previous definition, means "unknown language." "For he that speaketh in a tongue speaketh not unto men, but unto God: for no man understandeth *him....*" The word "him," again, is in italics and, again, should be deleted because "him" makes the Bible inaccurate. Acts 2:4-11, telling of the twelve apostles' receiving the gift from the Holy Spirit on the day of Pentecost, says that the apostles spoke

121

in tongues as the Spirit gave them utterance. The unconverted who heard them speak understood the tongues these twelve apostles were inspired to speak. The listeners reported that these apostles were speaking "the wonderful works of God." Therefore we know that the speaking in tongues was understood on Pentecost—not by the men speaking, but by those who heard them speak.

What you say when you speak in tongues is God's business, but *that* you do speak is your responsibility. On the day of Pentecost, as always, what the speaker spoke was an unknown language to himself, but not necessarily to the listeners. On Pentecost a group of listeners understood Peter, another group understood Matthew, and another group understood John, and so on with the other apostles. The possibility for a listener to understand the tongue is there, because God giveth the utterance. The Holy Spirit, God, gives it, but you by your own will must do the speaking.

> I Corinthians 14:2:
> For he that speaketh in...tongue speaketh not unto men, but unto [Whom?] God....

Another point in this scripture is that speakers speak to God. This does not negate the truth that the total message—tongues with interpretation—is going to be a message from God or for God to the people. Some may say that it is the man talking to God only. Let me ask you a question. When you say you spoke to the president on the telephone, what do you mean? You mean that when you spoke to him, he also talked to you. You did not do all the talking. This truth here in the Word is the same. Speaking to God is a two-way street. You talk to Him, and He talks to you. That is the essence of it.

Now, a point which must be studied and understood is that speaking in tongues in one's private prayer life edifies the speaker.

I Corinthians 14:4:
He that speaketh in...tongue edifieth himself....

In a believers' meeting I do the speaking in tongues, but as I speak God gives the utterance. Then I give the interpretation from God, which will edify the minds of the believers.

There are two basic ways whereby you may edify your mind: (1) study the Word and let it dwell richly in your mind; and (2) be in a believers' meeting where the speaking in tongues is interpreted, for the interpretation will give knowledge to your mind that will exhort and comfort.

When I bring forth a message in tongues with its interpretation, is my spirit edified? No. But my mind, as well as the minds of other people present, is edified. The mind of the Christian must be edified, because the mind—the thinking—makes a person what he is. The Bible says in Proverbs 23:7, "For as he thinketh in his heart, so *is* he...."

When a man of body, soul, and spirit speaks in tongues in his private prayer life or in a believers' meeting and he does not believe to interpret, his speaking in tongues will be a prayer or praise to God, and it will edify the spirit of the man who speaks. That is why verse 4 of I Corinthians 14 stipulates, "He that speaketh in an...tongue edifieth himself...." When we speak in tongues without interpretation, we edify the spirit that is in us which is called the inner man.

Now the problem that we run into is that some say the spirit of Christ in you is perfect; therefore, how can this speaking in tongues edify the spirit? Why does the spirit in a Christian need edifying? The spirit is just like a baby, which though perfect, still needs nurturing. So it is with the spirit in you; you feed it by speaking in tongues.

The underlying law involved in this whole matter is that God is Spirit and can speak to spirit only. Almost every group confuses flesh and spirit because they do not keep their Biblical principles straight. I know that the spirit is perfect. But Christians themselves become spiritually stagnant. They do not keep refreshed because many do not edify their spirits by speaking in tongues. In your private prayer life your spirit is edified, it is built up, it grows by speaking in tongues—not by interpretation, not by prophecy.

Interpretation and prophecy build up the body of believers, not in their spirits but in their minds.

> I Corinthians 14:5:
> I would that ye all spake with tongues, but rather that ye prophesied....

This is usually where people stop reading in order to say that speaking in tongues in the Church is not very important. They would rather have a believer prophesy. Most of the people who put forth this argument never prophesy either. Do you see the trickery of Satan? He wants to belittle the Word, chop the Word to pieces. There is nothing that equals speaking in tongues in your private life. This will build you up spiritually, whereas speaking in tongues with boldness in a believers' meeting with its interpretation builds up the body of believers.

> I Corinthians 14:5:
> I would that ye all spake with tongues, but rather that ye prophesied [in the Church]: for greater *is* he that prophesieth than he that speaketh with tongues, except he interpret, that the church may receive edifying.

When the believer speaks in tongues and interprets, the Church receives edifying. In the spirit? No. Where? In the mind. The interpretation is always in the language of the body of people present. This is why I Corinthians 14:3 says, "But he that prophesieth speaketh unto men...." Why? Because prophecy is in the language of the body of people present. So if the congregation were German, the prophecy would have to be in German.

I Corinthians 14:3:
But he that prophesieth speaketh unto men *to* edification, and exhortation, and comfort.

Therefore, when you speak in tongues and interpret or prophesy, you and the other believers present are edified by way of exhortation and comfort. In your own private life, who has to be blessed? You, the individual believer. In a believers' meeting, however, everyone must be edified.

I Corinthians 14:12:
Even so ye, forasmuch as ye are zealous of spiritual *gifts* [things or matters], seek that ye may excel to the edifying of the church.

The word "gifts" is in italics and should be deleted. The word "spiritual" is the word *pneumatikos,* meaning "things of the spirit." We must be zealous for things of the spirit, whether privately for our own selves spiritually or publicly for the minds of the entire body of believers. Let all things be done unto edifying!

Chapter Ten

HOW TO SPEAK IN TONGUES

Now that you know *why* one speaks in tongues and *when* one speaks in tongues, I know that you would like to receive into manifestation the power of the fullness of the Holy Spirit. I know that you would like to speak the wonderful works of God and magnify God. To do this, there is one thing you must do, and that is to believe God's Word. Surely you do believe God's Word, for what He has promised He is not only willing to perform, but He is able to perform. I can assure you upon the integrity of God's Word that when you speak in tongues you will be speaking the wonderful works of God and magnifying God.*

Before you can tap any of God's resources you must know, first of all, what is available. You know speaking in tongues is available

---

*Acts 2:11: "Cretes and Arabians, we do hear them speak in our tongues the wonderful works of God."

Acts 10:46: "For they heard them speak with tongues, and magnify God...."

because the Word of God says all born-again believers have the holy spirit within them, which is the ability to speak in tongues. Next you must know how to receive it, which is set forth in the following paragraphs.

Let me unfold the keys to you, and shortly you too will be speaking the wonderful works of God. Acts 2:4 says, "And they were all filled with the Holy Ghost...." They were all filled; nobody was missed. Nobody ever gets missed if he has heard the Word and if he believes it and then acts upon it. God is always faithful, and nobody then can be passed over. Do exactly what I tell you to do down to the most minute detail.

Paul, in I Thessalonians 2:13, thanked God that "when ye received the word of God which ye heard of us, ye received *it* not *as* the word of men, but as it is in truth, the word of God...." You too must follow God's truth as told in the Word of God. But if you think this is just Victor Paul Wierwille writing or speaking to you, you will never receive. If you know that what I am saying to you are words which the Holy Ghost has spoken and is speaking to you by me, then you too will manifest the greatness of the power of God. If you will *literally* do what I ask you, then you can manifest the fullness of the abundance of God, the wonderful power of God.

Remember Acts 2:4 says, "And they were all filled with the Holy Ghost, and [they] began to speak...." They, the people, did the speaking.

Have you ever thought through the mechanics of speech? You with your own vocal organs have to do the speaking. The same mechanics that are involved in speaking English or any other known language are involved in speaking in tongues. For instance, if I say, "I love the Lord Jesus Christ," what did I mechanically do? I moved my lips, I moved my tongue, I moved my throat, I made the sound, and I had to think. All this is involved in the mechanics of speech.

You say audibly, "I love the Lord Jesus Christ." What did you do? You moved your lips, your throat, and your tongue to speak. You formulated the words; you pushed them out.

The only difference between speaking in tongues and speaking in English is that when I say, "I love the Lord Jesus Christ," I have to think. When I speak in tongues, I do not think the words I speak. God gives the words to my spirit, and I formulate them on my lips. I do not think the words, but they are there when I move my lips, my throat, my tongue.

131

Believe to be very natural and at ease. You have to move your lips, your throat, your tongue; you push the air through your voice box to make the sounds. You have to formulate the words, but the words you speak, as in Acts 2:4, are as the Spirit gives you utterance. *What* you speak is God's business, but *that* you speak is your business. I make the sounds, but the words that I speak are given to my spirit. God gives the utterance, and they are words that magnify His name; they are speaking the wonderful works of God. This is the greatness of the manifestation of speaking in tongues.

If you understand the mechanics of speaking in English or in any other language that you know, then you understand the mechanics of speaking in tongues. If you are born again of God's Spirit, the power is in you, but you have to do the speaking—not God—you do it. You will have no difficulty with God; the only difficulty you will have is in your own mind and your understanding of what you have to do. You, not the Spirit, move your lips; you move your tongue; you move your throat; you give the words sound by the power of God that is in you. Thus you are speaking forth the wonderful, wonderful works of God. How simple and beautiful it really is.

Acts 2 is the order of action for the Church.

> Acts 2:38:
> Then Peter said unto them, Repent, and be baptized every one of you in the name of Jesus Christ for the remission of sins, and ye shall receive [*lambanō,** ye shall manifest] the gift of the Holy Ghost [*pneuma hagion*].

This is for the Church Age in which you and I live. When you confess with your mouth the Lord Jesus and believe that God raised him from the dead, you have the remission of sins.**

The Word says, "ye shall receive." You are to manifest in the senses world the proof that you have received spiritually. As you manifest, you speak the wonderful works of God; you magnify God.

---

*There are two Greek words for "receive" used in relation to receiving the holy spirit. *Dechomai* means "to receive the inherent power and ability." *Lambanō* means "to receive to the extent of outwardly manifesting."

**Romans 10:9: "That if thou shalt confess with thy mouth the Lord Jesus, and shalt believe in thine heart that God hath raised him from the dead, thou shalt be saved."

John 7 tells us a great truth that you and I need to understand when we manifest forth the power of the Holy Spirit.

> John 7:37 and 38:
> ...Jesus stood and cried, saying, If any man thirst, let him come unto me, and drink.
>
> He that believeth on me, as the scripture hath said, out of his belly shall flow rivers of living water.

The word "belly" stands for the depth of the soul of a man. "Out of the innermost being of that man shall flow rivers [not little streams] of living water." When you receive into manifestation the power from the Holy Spirit, you do not receive more spiritual substance; you just receive into evidence, into manifestation in the senses world, what you already spiritually have within. Manifesting the holy spirit does not mean you have been given something new; you are simply manifesting to your senses what you have within. The gift is already in you. God gave you the ability to speak in tongues when you were born again. The *act* of speaking in tongues is your responsibility; you already have the potential. If you don't speak in tongues, it isn't because God hasn't given you the ability. God through

134

His Son promised, "out of his belly shall flow rivers of living water."

This is what Jesus Christ spoke and what he told the apostles before he ascended. Out of their belly, out of their innermost being, would flow rivers of living water. So when you begin to speak in tongues, you formulate the words, you speak forth the words and let them bubble; let them flow freely, not trickle. When you start speaking in tongues, let it flow with one sound right after the other. That is what the Word says, and that is what it means.

> Luke 11:11:
> If a son shall ask bread of any of you that is a father, will he give him a stone? or if *he ask* a fish, will he for a fish give him a serpent?

Suppose you had a son who was hungry, and you had bread in your house. If he asked for it, would you give him a stone? I am sure you would not.

> Verses 12 and 13:
> Or if he shall ask an egg, will he offer him a scorpion?

135

> If ye then [as fathers], being evil, know how to give good gifts unto your children: how much more shall *your* heavenly Father give the Holy Spirit to them that ask him?

The word "ask" is the same word as "demand." Do you know why you can demand payment on a check? Because the money behind it is already in the bank. All you have to do is walk up to the cashier's window and ask for the money for that check. "...How much more shall *your* heavenly Father give the Holy Spirit to them that ask [demand it of] him?" Why can we demand the holy spirit? Because it already has been given to us.

I want to call one more thing to your attention. The fullest cargoes of life come in on quiet seas. When the oceans are rough, the ships lay out in the deep; but when the oceans quiet down, the great cargo ships come into the harbor. The greatest cargoes of our spiritual life come in over our quiet inner seas. One of the things that the Word of God has done to me is to give peace to me on the inside so that I can receive the abundance of the power of the fullness of God.

Galatians 3:5:
He therefore that ministereth to you the

Spirit, and worketh miracles among you, *doeth he it* by the works of the law, or by the hearing of faith?

How do I minister the holy spirit to people? Do I do this by the hearing of faith? Yes! I do not do this by the works of the law.

I am ministering the holy spirit to you, teaching you exactly what to do. After you have read my instructions, I want you to close your eyes and sit quietly. Remember that when I have ministered the holy spirit to you, I want you to move your lips, your throat, your tongue. You make the sounds.

Sit quietly and do exactly as I instruct. Remember the Word of God says in Job 29:23, "...and they opened their mouth wide *as* for the latter rain." To drink, you have to open your mouth. In John 20:22 Jesus instructed the apostles before the ascension to breathe in. He opened his mouth wide, and he breathed in.* In a moment I want you to open your mouth wide and breathe in.

While you are sitting, follow this instruction. Open your mouth wide and breathe in. You are

---

*See page 141 explanation of John 20:22.

not going to receive anything more spiritually; you are now going to manifest the spirit's presence. Just breathe in. Open your mouth wide. While you are breathing in, thank God for having filled you with the fullness of the power of His holy spirit. Don't beg Him; thank Him for it.

When you begin to speak in tongues, move your lips, your throat, your tongue. Speak forth. When you have finished one sound, speak another. Do not pay any attention to what you are thinking. You formulate the words; you move your lips, your throat, your tongue; you say it. You are magnifying God no matter what the words sound like to your ears. It is your part to speak in tongues; it is God's part to give the utterance.

Keep moving your lips, your throat and tongue. Formulate another sound. You have to formulate the sounds differently on your lips. God has given them to your spirit. They are in your spirit coming on your tongue; you have to speak them out. You are speaking the wonderful works of God; you are magnifying God; you are speaking in tongues. The external manifestation is your proof in the senses world that you have Christ within. Get bold in it; let it flow out; let it effervesce. "Out of his belly shall flow rivers of living water." Keep on speaking. God is giving the words to your spirit; your spirit is bringing them up to your throat, and you are bringing them out.

"Father, in the name of Jesus Christ and by the power of God that is within me, I now minister the fullness of your holy spirit into manifestation in this believer's life." Breathe in deeply, and now begin to speak in tongues as I have just instructed you.

Isn't God wonderful!

If you can speak one word, you can speak ten thousand words; because if you can speak one word, you have the power, the God-given ability, to speak more. Every time you speak, remember that you are edifying yourself spiritually, building yourself up. You are speaking the wonderful works of God; you are magnifying God. You have the proof now in the senses world that you have Christ within, that you are a joint heir with him.

In a moment I want you to speak again, to speak once more so that you become fluent and confident from experience. To learn another language by using your mind would take months; but to speak in unknown tongues happens instantly. God knows the tongues, so He gives them to your spirit and you speak them forth.

Anybody who knows even the slightest bit about languages knows that "beep, beep, beep, boop, boop, boop" would not be speaking in tongues. Speaking in tongues is speaking a developed language. Now once more I want you to speak in tongues. Just get quiet. Move your lips, throat, and tongue, and start speaking again. Keep on speaking. You are speaking the wonderful works of God, magnifying God. You now have proved to your senses that Christ is in you and that you have the power of the holy spirit. This is the greatness of God's wonderful power to you as a believer.

Chapter Eleven

FILLED TO OVERFLOWING

Just before Jesus Christ ascended, as recorded in John 20, he instructed his disciples about a new dimension of their glorious walk which would come to pass on the day of Pentecost.

John 20:22:
And when he had said this, he breathed on *them* [The word "them" is incorrectly supplied in the King James Version and should be deleted. The word "on" is the word "in." He breathed in.], and saith unto them, Receive ye the Holy Ghost [The Greek text uses the words *lambanō pneuma hagion,** "bring into manifestation holy spirit."].

---

*The Giver is *pneuma hagion,* Holy Spirit; the gift is *pneuma hagion,* holy spirit. For a detailed study of the usage of these two Greek words in the Bible, as well as the Greek words *lambanō* and *dechomai,* read Victor Paul Wierwille, *Receiving the Holy Spirit Today,* 7th ed. (New Knoxville, Ohio: American Christian Press, 1982), pp. xiii–xxii, 225–296.

At the first hour of prayer on the day of Pentecost when the apostles "breathed in," they confessed with their mouth the Lord Jesus believing God had raised him from the dead, and thus were born again of God's Spirit and spiritually filled to capacity. The word "receive," *lambanō,* indicates that the apostles manifested the gift they had just received spiritually in all of its overflowing fullness.

To be born of the Spirit—to be born again or to be born from above—is to be spiritually filled to capacity (*plēroō*), while the fullness in manifestation of that birth is to be filled to overflowing (*plēthō*). Salvation brings *plēroō,* a capacity fullness; manifesting the holy spirit brings *plēthō,* overflowing fullness. This study is basically focused on *plēroō* and *plēthō* which describe every facet of knowledge available to us regarding the new birth.

Plēthō is a later form of the word *pimplēmi,* a derivative of *pleos.* Both *plēroō* and *plēthō* are derivatives of the basic root word *pleos,* which means "filled." *Pimplēmi* meant "to fill to capacity and overflow." In Greek literature, *pimplēmi* is used of a river overflowing its banks. It is also used in describing the full moon when it is overflowing in all of its brilliance. *Plēroō* means "to fill only to normal capacity," like a river filled in its natural or normal flow; *plētho* means "to fill to overflowing in abundance."

> Luke 1:57:
> Now Elisabeth's full [*pimplēmi, plēthō*] time came that she should be delivered; and she brought forth a son.

Elisabeth was *plēthō,* for she delivered the child—the delivery is the overflowing.

> Colossians 2:9:
> For in him [Christ] dwelleth all the fulness [*plērōma,* from *plēroō,* full to capacity] of the Godhead bodily.

Christ was filled to capacity with the fullness of the Godhead. The fullness of God overflowing *out* of Jesus Christ made it possible for Jesus to say, "He that hath seen me hath seen the Father." Jesus Christ declared the Father; he made known God. Jesus was overflowing with God's presence, power, and Word, and thereby declared God.

Another example dealing with "being filled," besides the two Greek words *plēroō* and *plēthō,* should help to clarify our subject.

> Matthew 5:6:
> Blessed *are* they which do hunger and thirst after righteousness: for they shall be filled [*chortazō*].

> Matthew 14:20:
> And they did all eat, and were filled [*chortazō*]. . . .

The word "filled," *chortazō,* is the Greek word used in both instances in Matthew. This kind of "filling," *chortazō,* has variations depending upon the appetite of the individual being filled.

There is an illustration that teaches the new birth and the manifestations very beautifully. Assume that a glass represents the natural man; the liquid inside the glass represents spirit. When the spirit comes in (when a man confesses with his mouth the Lord Jesus believing God raised him from the dead), this man of body and soul is filled (*plēroō*) to normal capacity in his whole being. This is the new-birth filling, "he breathed in." Then "Receive ye [*lambanō*, receive to the degree of manifesting]" is to be filled (*plēthō*), which is the overflowing fullness. Biblically, the filling with the new birth (*plēroō*) is always to be associated with the overflowing (*plēthō*) in manifestation.

144

On the day of the ascension Jesus spoke to the twelve apostles.

> Acts 1:5:
> For John truly baptized with water; but ye shall be baptized with [in] the Holy Ghost [holy spirit, the gift] not many days hence.

The "baptized with holy spirit" is the filling of the new birth, *plēroō,* filled to capacity.

> Acts 1:8:
> But ye shall receive [*lambanō,* you shall overflow, *plēthō,* manifest] power, after that the Holy Ghost is come upon you: and ye [then] shall be witnesses unto me both in Jerusalem, and in all Judaea, and in Samaria, and unto the uttermost part of the earth.

The overflow comes with the operation of the manifestations of the spirit.

> John 7:38 and 39:
> He that believeth on me, as the scripture hath said, out of his belly shall flow rivers of living water.
>
> (But this spake he of the Spirit, which they that believe on him should receive [*lambanō,*

receive into manifestation]: for the Holy Ghost was not yet *given;* because that Jesus was not yet glorified.)

The word "belly" in verse 38 is the figure of speech *metonymy,** meaning "innermost being." The word "flow" is *rheusousin* from the root word *rheō*. The obsolete form of *rheō* meant "to speak." From this same root comes the word *rhēma,* meaning "that which is spoken." "Out of his innermost being shall be spoken rivers (not trickles) of living water."

This relates directly to the fullness (*plēthō*) of the holy spirit as seen in verse 39. The giving of the gift, the new birth, the filling with the spirit, Christ in you, was on the day of Pentecost.

The historical events of Pentecost, including the new birth with its various overflowing attributes, are recorded in Acts 2.

Acts 2:1,2,4:
And when the day of Pentecost was fully [*sumplēroō*] come, they were all with one accord in one place.

---

*This figure of speech is used when the container is put for the contents—"belly" used for "innermost being."

And suddenly there came a sound from heaven as of a rushing mighty wind [heavy breathing*], and it [their breathing in] filled [*plēroō*] all the house where they were sitting.

And they were all filled [*plēthō*] with the Holy Ghost, and began to speak with other tongues, as the Spirit gave them utterance.

The word "filled" in verse 2 is *plēroō,* meaning "filled to capacity." As the disciples breathed in, the sound of their breathing filled to capacity, *plēroō,* the Temple. The disciples were filled to capacity, *plēroō,* as they breathed in because verse 4 says they were all filled, *plēthō,* and began to speak (the overflowing), one of the nine manifestations of the spirit.

If language would permit, God could have taken the first four verses of Acts 2 and condensed them into one, for the new birth and the manifestations are to be as one. The filling of the apostles of verse 2 is *plēroō,* the inherent, new-birth filling; the filling in verse 4 is *plēthō,* the external manifestation, or the overflowing of the inherent filling. The manifestations of the

---

*J. N. Darby, *The New Testament: A New Translation from the Revised Text of the Greek Original.* 2d ed. rev. (London: G. Morrish, n.d.). *Pnoēs* is not "wind," but "as of a hard breathing."

spirit are the overflowing power in the life of the believer which in turn produces the fruit of the spirit of love, joy, peace, long-suffering, gentleness, goodness, faith (faithfulness), meekness, and temperance.

Beginning on Pentecost and effective thereafter, believers immediately upon being born again of God's Spirit were to overflow. They were to not only have the natural, normal filling to capacity, *plēroō,* but also the overflowing, *plēthō.* The Apostle Peter demonstrates such an example.

> Acts 4:8:
> Then Peter, filled [*plēthō*] with the Holy Ghost [the gift of holy spirit]....

Peter was filled to overflowing, expressed by the usage of the word *plēthō* rather than *plēroō,* operating all nine of the manifestations. Thereby Peter knew all those matters recorded in Acts 4, which are a continuation of the activities recorded in Acts 3.

After Acts 4:8 documents that Peter was filled with the holy spirit, Acts 4 continues by telling of events that occurred to Peter and John.

Acts 4:31:
And when they had prayed, the place was shaken where they were assembled together; and they were all filled [*plēthō*] with the Holy Ghost....

The assembled people were filled to overflowing. Because of the manifestations of the spirit, namely speaking in tongues, interpretation of tongues, and prophecy, that prayer meeting was genuinely powerful and edifying to the believers, all of whom were exhorted and comforted. It does not say in Acts 4:31 that the believers were refilled. There is never a leaking out of the spirit or a need for a second filling. The believer is always filled (*plēroō*) to normal capacity; but the filling to overflowing (*plēthō*) begins when the believer initiates the manifestations.

Acts 8 contains the first record in the history of the Christian Church of new Christians' being born again without immediately manifesting the holy spirit. Because this Samaritan group did not manifest, Peter and John were summoned from Jerusalem. Acts 8 tells of the course these two apostles pursued to remedy the situation.

Acts 8:15:
Who, when they were come down, prayed for them, that they might receive [*lambanō,* manifest] the Holy Ghost [holy spirit, the gift].

The believers in Samaria were filled (*plēroō*), but they were not filled (*plēthō*) to the end that they were manifesting the holy spirit.

Verse 16:
(For as yet he [holy spirit] was fallen upon none of them: only they were baptized in the name of the Lord Jesus.)

To be baptized in the name of the Lord Jesus has nothing to do with water but everything to do with being filled (*plēroō*), having Christ in you, the hope of glory, which is the new birth.

Although the Samaritans had received the new birth, they had not as yet been filled to overflowing. The usage of the phrase "as yet he was fallen upon none of them" means grammatically and Biblically that the spirit was not overflowing in manifestation.

Verse 17:
Then laid they [Peter and John] *their* hands
on them, and they received [*lambanō,* they
manifested *pneuma hagion*] the Holy Ghost
[the gift, holy spirit].

With this, the gift started overflowing, run-
ning over on the outside.

Another example of "salvation fullness" coming before "manifestation overflow" is recorded
in Acts 9 in the account of young Saul (whose
Greek name is Paul).

Acts 9:17:
And Ananias went his way, and entered into
the house; and putting his hands on him
[Paul] said, Brother Saul, the Lord, *even*
Jesus, that appeared unto thee in the way
as thou camest, hath sent me, that thou
mightest receive thy sight, and be filled
[*plēthō,* overflow] with the Holy Ghost
[*pneuma hagion,* holy spirit, the gift].

Paul confessed the Lord Jesus as his savior
on the road to Damascus, but he did not overflow, he did not receive, *lambanō,* into manifestation. When Ananias came into the house of
Judas to minister to Paul, he called Paul "Brother

Saul," indicating that Saul was a spiritual brother. Ananias's purpose for visiting Paul was "that thou mightest receive thy sight, and be filled [*plēthō*] with the Holy Ghost." Paul was born again (*dechomai, plēroō,* filled to capacity), but he was not filled to an overflowing abundance (*lambanō, plēthō*) until Ananias ministered to him. Paul soon overflowed with the manifestations of the spirit, however, for I Corinthians 14:18 says of Paul, "I thank my God, I speak with tongues more than ye all."

Acts 10 informs us about Peter's ministering for the first time to a Gentile household—the house of Cornelius in Caesarea.

> Acts 10:44-46:
> While Peter yet spake these words, the Holy Ghost [*pneuma hagion,* holy spirit, the gift] fell on all them which heard the word.
>
> And they of the circumcision which believed were astonished, as many as came with Peter, because that on the Gentiles also was poured out the gift of the Holy Ghost [*pneuma hagion*].
>
> For they heard them speak with tongues, and magnify God....

The overflowing, indicating the operation of the manifestations, is evidenced by the words "poured out." The last verse quoted specifically informs us that the overflowing was manifested by speaking in tongues: "For they heard them speak with tongues."

Acts 11 contains Peter's defense of his actions in going to the house of Cornelius and there presenting Christ and his gospel to the Gentiles for the first time.

> Acts 11:15:
> And as I [Peter] began to speak, the Holy Ghost [*pneuma hagion,* holy spirit, the gift] fell on them, as on us at the beginning.

Just as we saw earlier in John's and Peter's experience in Samaria, according to Acts 19, Paul had the same experience at Ephesus. He found disciples who were born again, who were filled to capacity (*plēroō*) spiritually, but lacked the overflowing (*plēthō*).

> Acts 19:6:
> And when Paul had laid *his* hands upon them, the Holy Ghost [*pneuma hagion,* holy spirit, the gift] came on them; and they spake with tongues....

Again, this is a fullness to overflowing by people in the Church, born again of God's Spirit.

Ephesians 5 contains an interesting usage of the word *plēroō*. Again it refers to that depth of quietness to which we are to be filled.

> Ephesians 5:18:
> And be not drunk with wine...but be filled [*plēroō*] with the Spirit.

This verse indicates to us that "filled with the Spirit" is the new birth—Christ in you, the hope of glory. Be filled, *plēroō,* in the innermost part of you, which is Christ in you, to capacity.

Let us observe the usage of the Greek word *plēthō,* filled to overflowing, in a few other scriptures which do not deal specifically with the new birth.

> Luke 1:41:
> And it came to pass, that, when Elisabeth heard the salutation of Mary, the babe leaped in her womb; and Elisabeth was filled [*plēthō,* overflowed] with the Holy Ghost [*pneuma hagion,* holy spirit].

Elisabeth was "filled to overflowing," demonstrated by her giving a word of prophecy, as the following verses in Luke 1 disclose.

Luke 1 also tells of Elisabeth's husband, the father of John the Baptist.

> Luke 1:67:
> And his father Zacharias was filled [*plēthō,* overflowed] with the Holy Ghost [*pneuma hagion*], and [he] prophesied....

Zacharias was filled to overflowing. He prophesied.

On the lake Gennesaret, Luke 5 records that Jesus told Simon to let down his "nets for a draught."

> Luke 5:7:
> And they beckoned unto *their* partners, which were in the other ship, that they should come and help them. And they came, and filled [*plēthō,* overflowed] both the ships, so that they began to sink.

They had so many fish in the boats that the boats were full to overflowing and sinking.

There can obviously be no overflow until a vessel is filled to capacity. We note in Acts 6:3 that when seven men were elected from among the disciples, the Word says, "Wherefore, brethren, look ye out among you seven men of honest report, full [*plērēs*—adjective form of *plēroō*] of the Holy Ghost [*pneuma hagion*]...." They were men filled to capacity. Acts 7:55 says, "But he [Stephen], being full [*plērēs*] of the Holy Ghost,..." filled to capacity.

Acts 5 also gives an account of the apostles teaching in Jerusalem.

Acts 5:28:
Saying...behold, ye [the apostles] have filled [*plēroō*] Jerusalem with your doctrine....

The apostles' doctrine had penetrated Jerusalem to the point that the city was "filled to capacity" with the Word.

Colossians 1 contains a wonderful prayer for believers—to be filled to capacity.

Colossians 1:9:
For this cause we also, since the day we heard *it* [your love in the spirit], do not

cease to pray for you, and to desire that ye might be filled [*plēroō*] with the knowledge of his will in all wisdom and spiritual understanding.

Be filled to full capacity. This is my prayer for you and all of God's people. I desire it to be your prayer for me also, that we might be filled to full capacity "with the knowledge of his will" and then overflowing with the abundance thereof.

The only way we can have a knowledge of God's will is to know God's Word. To be filled with the knowledge of His will in all wisdom and spiritual understanding is first and primary for every believer. Then the overflowing will be a mighty blessing. This is how the teachings of the apostles penetrated all of Jerusalem. The whole city became filled to capacity with the Word of God because the knowledge of God's Word was dwelling within the apostles, and they overflowed (*plēthō*) as they spoke that Word of God with boldness, operating the manifestations of the spirit, especially speaking in tongues.

PART IV

THE CHURCH
TODAY

PART IV

THE CHURCH TODAY

The Church of Grace since its founding on the day of Pentecost has been endowed with the power of the holy spirit. Yet the first-century Church was a church on the move, something we have not seen in our lifetimes. The Bible says that God does not change. If God hasn't changed, then why the difference between the early Church and the present Church? "The First-Century Church in the Twentieth" studies the early Church so that we can apply its strengths to the twentieth-century Church and, like it, also prosper.

An obvious weakness in the current church is its lack of unity. "Why Division?" examines this aspect of the modern church to see where we are limiting God's power because we are not of one mind.

The Church of Grace regardless of time is made up of the members of the Body of Christ. No building or denominational label qualifies as a church in God's eyes.

Only as the called-out ones band together on the accuracy of God's Word and fully mature by following the accurate Word can we ever hope to help ourselves and help others, and thus live the more abundant life.

Chapter Twelve

THE FIRST-CENTURY CHURCH IN THE TWENTIETH

The first-century Church had tremendous power because Christians believed that when they were saved they received the power from the Holy Spirit and thus could operate the nine manifestations of the spirit. Besides having such internal power, the early believers studied the Word of God and acted on it as being the will of God.

The first-century Church, as the record in the Book of Acts indicates, made tremendous progress. It moved with an anointing such as we have never seen. The fact that they progressed beyond the point which the current Church has achieved cannot be accredited to God because God has not changed. When some people talk about God pouring out a special anointing in these last days, it simply is not true. The Word says He sent His gift on the day of Pentecost. His gift is here. The early

Church obviously was more alive and dynamic, not because God was more powerful, but because it operated more effectively.

The early Church, the Body, as recorded in the Book of Acts and the Church Epistles, developed a pattern for its growth in various localities:

1. Each person was responsible to witness *with boldness* to the Word of God. When a person accepted Jesus Christ as his lord, "older" Christians continued to nurture and shepherd him until the new Christian was grounded well enough to stand and walk alone on that Word.

2. Small supervised meetings, called churches, were held in private homes with a head elder or pastor overseeing each home unit.

3. Personal revisits and written communications were kept up with each group, each church, by apostles, prophets, evangelists, pastors, and teachers.

4. Christians were not to be sidetracked by material possessions. Thus they sold their unneeded possessions in order to further the work of the ministry.

The early Church was born into a society which was just as indoctrinated and hardened as any society has been at any time. The Romans were governmentally in control, and paganism was rampant. Yet the first-century Christian Church turned the world upside down—which means they turned it right side up. They had the potential spiritual ability, which became kinetic in a most wonderful and dynamic way. Within one generation the early believers changed the whole spiritual and moral climate of that part of the world. We do not know how many Christians really walked on the Word of God in the first century and witnessed to the then-known world, but we do know that according to Acts 19:10, in two years and three months "all...Asia [currently known as Asia Minor] heard the word of the Lord Jesus, both Jews [Judeans] and Greeks."

This feat certainly could not have been accomplished, and was not accomplished, by one man. But under Paul's ministry and teaching, the original "about twelve"* men (households) were inspired and learned to walk on the Word of God and share it with others. All Asia Minor heard this wonderful Word of God as it spread out from Ephesus because each believer endeavored to win one and nurtured that one until the newborn Christian was strong enough

---

*Acts 19:7: "And all the men were about twelve."

to stand and walk on the Word of God, operating the manifestations of the spirit. All this was accomplished without the modern aids of radio, television, and printed matter.

One of the earliest accounts of a believer winning a friend is found in John 1:40 and 41. This is the record in which Andrew first found his brother Peter and brought him to the lord.

As in our day, not everyone in the first century believed and was saved when a Christian witnessed. When you preach the Word of God and share it with an individual or with a group, you will discover that the response will be as in Acts 28:24, "And some believed the things which were spoken, and some believed not."

In the unbelieving group, of course, were those who according to Acts 17:32, when they heard the Word of God regarding the resurrection of the dead, "...some mocked: and others said, We will hear thee again of this *matter.*"

The early Church leaders, including Peter and the other apostles, were very bold in the presentation of the Word of God; and because of their boldness, multitudes of both men and women were added to the Church, as Acts 5:14 tells, "And believers were the more added to the

Lord, multitudes both of men and women." However as the record in Acts 5 continues, the high priest and the Sadducees laid their hands on the apostles and put them in prison. Yet as soon as the Christians were released, God told them, "Go, stand and speak in the temple to the people all the words of this life." So they went back into the Temple to teach.

The high priest soon came also to the Temple and called the Sanhedrin together to bring the prisoners before it; but the apostles were not in the prison. When the high priest, the captain of the Temple, and the chief priests (according to Acts 5:24) heard what God was doing and how He had released these men from prison, they were disturbed. They did not want the growth of this new movement. It took great courage on the part of the apostles to go into the Temple again and teach the people, knowing ahead of time there would be trouble when they spoke the true Word of God. According to verse 29, "...Peter and the *other* apostles answered and said, We ought to obey God rather than men."

After they had been ruthlessly interrogated, the apostles were beaten and commanded not to speak in the name of Jesus. Yet the apostles persevered, for Acts 5:42 says, "And daily in the

167

temple, and in every house, they ceased not to teach and preach Jesus Christ."

Those in the synagogues could not tolerate them, even as the true believers on the Word of God in many places cannot be tolerated in the organized and established churches today. This necessitated the second point in this study, namely, small supervised meetings, called churches, in the homes. I will give you the scriptures I have noted so you can read exactly what is written in the Word of God concerning such meetings.

In Acts 5 we read that the apostles went from house to house talking to the people about the Word of the Lord. This is the first record demonstrating how the apostles declared the Word of God very early in the age of the Church to which you and I belong.

Later, in Acts 8:3 we read that Paul (whose Hebrew name was Saul), before being saved, entered "into every house, and haling men and women committed *them* to prison." It was necessary to go into the houses to find the Christians since these were their meeting places.

Acts 10 is the first record of a Gentile household coming into the experience of the new birth and receiving the power from the Holy Spirit into manifestation.

> Acts 10:2:
> *A* devout *man* [Cornelius], and one that feared [respected] God with all his house....

This meeting, again in a house, was characteristic of the early Church.

Acts 16 tells of Paul's and Silas's ministering in a house immediately after God had released them from prison. The keeper of the prison spoke in Acts 16:30, "...Sirs, what must I do to be saved?"

> Acts 16:31 and 32:
> And they said, Believe on the Lord Jesus Christ, and thou shalt be saved, and thy house.
>
> And they spake unto him the word of the Lord, and to all that were in his house.

This is a significant verse of scripture in that the precedent is set for witnessing to entire households at one time. We are not to attempt to win just one person out of a household for the Lord Jesus Christ, but we should endeavor

169

to win the whole house: father, mother, and all the children.

The culture of the East differs from the culture in America, but we can at least apply the principles of the Word. If we can convince father and mother, I feel confident that the younger children can be won, especially if the father and mother are taught the accuracy of the Word of God concerning their responsibility toward God and their families.

> Acts 18:8:
> And Crispus, the chief ruler of the synagogue, believed on the Lord with all his house; and many of the Corinthians hearing believed, and were baptized.

The head of the house was converted; he was taught the accuracy of the Word of God, and in turn the entire household was brought into the household of faith, receiving the faith of the Lord Jesus Christ.

Another example of a house as a meeting place is recorded in Acts 21.

> Acts 21:8:
> And the next *day* we that were of Paul's

company departed, and came unto Caesarea: and we entered into the house of Philip the evangelist....

Philip's house had become a meeting place for the believers. Paul's lodging place in Rome also became a meeting place for the extension of the Word of God and the teaching of it in the early days of the Christian Church.

Acts 28:23,30,31:
And when they had appointed him a day, there came many to him into *his* lodging; to whom he expounded and testified the kingdom of God, persuading them concerning Jesus, both out of the law of Moses, and *out of* the prophets, from morning till evening.

And Paul dwelt two whole years in his own hired house, and received all that came in unto him,

Preaching the kingdom of God, and teaching those things which concern the Lord Jesus Christ, with all confidence, no man forbidding him.

This is the record of the early Church in the Book of Acts, which is the historical presentation of the founding and growth of the Christian Church.

Turn to Romans 16:3 and 5 and note that Paul sent word to the Romans saying, "Greet Priscilla and Aquila...*greet* the church [the local Christian group] that is in their house...."

> I Corinthians 1:11:
> For it hath been declared unto me of you, my brethren, by them *which are of the house* of Chloe, that there are contentions among you.

I Corinthians and Colossians give other examples of local Christian groups meeting in a house.

> I Corinthians 16:19:
> The churches of Asia salute you. Aquila and Priscilla salute you much in the Lord, with the church that is in their house.

> Colossians 4:15:
> Salute the brethren which are in Laodicea, and Nymphas, and the church which is in his house.

A verse in I Timothy ought to be read very carefully.

> I Timothy 3:15:
> But if I tarry long, that thou mayest know how thou oughtest to behave thyself in the house of God, which is the church of the living God, the pillar and ground of the truth.

The homes in which the churches met were called houses of God. These homes were the pillars of the Church, for these fellowships were built on the foundation of truth.

> Philemon 2:
> And to *our* beloved Apphia, and Archippus our fellowsoldier, and to the church in thy house.

Since these verses which I have shared with you are the Word of God concerning the early churches meeting in houses under proper supervision, this *must* be God's method of winning men and women to the Church and sustaining them. If you say the times have changed, then I would like to say the Word of God has not changed. When the churches met in the homes,

173

the small groups made possible participation by everyone, as well as the giving of attention and help to the individual.

Inside the home or church group there must be leadership. The work of the Lord cannot be done haphazardly. I believe we could meet in homes, in groups of six to possibly twenty people or so, depending on the size of the room. Then we could take care of the believers in every particular area. No one would need to drive very far, and yet the people would hear the wonderful Word of God. Our children could meet in a separate room with an adult teaching them the Word of God, or they could sit with the adults. Hearing the Word of God properly explained and the manifestations operated would be the greatest thing that could be done for them. Remember, it is the churches, the fellowships of believers, that we are concerned about; nothing that man has built will suffice.

Regarding elders or pastors for each unit, let us look at Paul's example in Ephesus as recorded in Acts 20. Paul calls the elders of the Ephesian church together to admonish them.

> Acts 20:28 and 29:
> Take heed therefore unto yourselves [which

is the first requirement of any leader], and to all the flock, over the which the Holy Ghost hath made you overseers, to feed the church of God, which he hath purchased with his own blood.

For I know this, that after my departing shall grievous wolves enter in among you, not sparing the flock.

The "overseer" refers to an elder who was the ruler, the leader, the supervisor in the house, the church. These elders were pastors for the local units, sometimes called bishops. The overseers must be very, very careful as to what goes on in the house where the church, the fellowship, is meeting.

Verse 30:
Also of your own selves shall men arise, speaking perverse things, to draw away disciples after them.

In other words, Satan would trick some from among the overseers themselves. There would be splits in the churches which were held in the homes because people were full of pride and wanted to draw away disciples after themselves and not after the Word of God. Therefore strong, accurate leadership was essential.

And this leadership was not determined by chance. The overseer was chosen by the man of God who was led by the Holy Spirit.

> Titus 1:5:
> For this cause left I thee in Crete, that thou shouldest set in order the things that are wanting, and ordain elders in every city, as I had appointed thee.

The elders were told how to behave in I Peter.

> I Peter 5:2 and 3:
> Feed the flock of God which is among you, taking the oversight *thereof,* not by constraint, but willingly; not for filthy lucre, but of a ready mind;
>
> Neither as being lords over *God's* heritage, but being ensamples to the flock.

Now, regarding the revisits by the apostles, prophets, evangelists, pastors, and teachers, the Book of Acts constantly tells of Paul's starting fellowships at various places and then revisiting them. We see other men—Timothy, Titus, Silvanus, and others—revisiting churches, fellowships. As we study the missionary journeys, we note that Derbe, Caesarea, Antioch of

Pisidia, Tarsus, Iconium, Pessinus, Ephesus, Troas, Neapolis, Philippi, Amphipolis, Apollonia, Thessalonica, Berea, Athens, and Corinth were among places revisited.

In Acts 20 we have the record of Paul's return visit to Ephesus where he called the elders of the church together. The reason there were elders (plural) in the church is that there were many houses where the people met, each house being under the supervision of an elder. Paul is speaking in the following verse to the elders in Ephesus.

> Acts 20:20:
> ...I kept back nothing that was profitable *unto you,* but have shewed you, and have taught you publickly [that is, in group meetings in large houses], and from house to house.

The Apostle Paul not only went from house to house to teach the wonderful Word of God, he also wrote letters to the scattered churches, local fellowships, which made up the Church, the Body. These letters were then read in the various homes where the Christians were meeting. This is how the early Church received instruction and grew. You will note that I and II Timothy specify the entire procedure and conduct for the leaders in relation to the Church. We cannot read these epistles too carefully because in them we find the truth which we need to know to accurately manifest the greatness of God's Word.

The fourth point in accounting for the rapid growth of the early Church was that Christians gave all material possessions which they did not need to the furthering of the Christian ministry. But before looking at this specific point, let us build up to it in Acts 4 to see the other "growth elements" which came before Christians gave up their excess material possessions.

According to Acts 4 Peter and John had just ministered healing to a man who was more than forty years old, for which deed they were imprisoned and charged not to speak at all and not to teach in the name of Jesus.* Upon their release from prison, however, Peter and John immediately began preaching the Word again.

> Acts 4:29:
> And now, Lord, behold their [the synagogue leaders'] threatenings: and grant unto thy

---

*Acts 4:18: "And they called them, and commanded them not to speak at all nor teach in the name of Jesus."

servants, that with all boldness they may speak thy word.

Isn't that a wonderful prayer? This is the first recorded prayer of the early Church. The apostles had been incarcerated, humiliated, hurt, and threatened for their teaching and for the way in which they ministered healing. Yet, when Peter and John returned to the group of believers— instead of asking for a vacation, instead of asking for an easier place to serve—they prayed, "Lord, behold their threatenings: and grant unto thy servants, that with all boldness they may speak thy word." Speaking the Word got them in trouble to begin with, but only their perseverance would further their mission.

The early Church always preached the Word and nothing but the Word—no private opinions. They spoke the Word with boldness, and often when they spoke the Word, they got into trouble. The question is, are we teaching the Word?

When we really present the Word of God and walk in the light of the Word of God, we may get persecution here and there. But this should not deter us. We should simply say, "Well, if Satan is trying so hard to obstruct our efforts, we must be doing something worthwhile. If our goals weren't worth anything, Satan wouldn't bother to intrude. He fights because we are battling him."

Notice that the disciples prayed, "...grant unto thy servants...." These men were sons of God in their heavenly relationship; but in their earthly responsibilities, they were to serve God, and thus they were called servants.

> Acts 4:31 and 32:
> And when they had prayed, the place was shaken where they were assembled together; and they were all filled with the Holy Ghost [*pneuma hagion*], and they spake the word of God with boldness.
>
> And the multitude of them [The text is "every one of them."] that believed were of one heart and of one soul: neither said any *of them* that ought of the things which he possessed was his own; but they had all things common.

Think of this in the early Church! All persons who were born again of God's Spirit and filled with power from the Holy Spirit were of one heart and of one soul. They had the Word, and they agreed on the Word. This is what gave the early Church power.

In studying "they had all things common," there are three words translated "common" from the critical Greek texts. The word used here in verse 32 means "to the end that in their believing and in their action they were commonly united." None of the things—the plurality—which a person possessed were really his own. The plurality that he possessed was common as far as need was concerned.

When the early Church began to move, all plurality that the members possessed was common among them. If a member had a need, the plurality was used to meet that need.

Verses 33-35:

And with great power gave the apostles witness of the resurrection of the Lord Jesus: and great grace [divine favor] was upon them all.

Neither was there any among them that lacked: for as many as were possessors [plural] of lands [plural] or houses [plural] sold them, and brought the prices of the things that were sold,

And laid *them* down at the apostles' feet: and distribution was made unto every man according as he had need.

Notice that the last word in Acts 4:35 is not "greed," but "need." There were people in the Church who had more than they needed of food, clothing, and shelter. Therefore, they sold their plurality—that which they did not need—to help someone else in the Church who had a need. Suppose there was a young couple in the Church, dedicated to the Lord, who loved His Word and wanted to start farming; they had a need. The Church was to help the couple get started.

In verse 34 carefully note the words "as many as were possessors." When these people who were possessors of lands (plural) and houses (plural) were born again, what did they do? They sold their plurality. They sold that which they did not need. Plurality is greed, not need. If we want the Church to move under the anointing of the power from the Holy Spirit as the early Church moved, we must be obedient to the Word of God and conquer our greed. Excesses weight us down, and Christians are not to be bogged down with matters of this world.

God never asked a man at any place in the Bible to sell or dispose of that which he needed for his livelihood. They sold that which they did not need, their plurality, and brought the money to the apostles, who distributed according to the need of the individual believer. One man's need may be more than another's. Every person must determine his need within himself, according to the renewing of his own mind after being born again.

You may ask, "Well, who would you trust with the collected possessions?" Whom did the early Church trust with them? The apostles. If you as a Christian do not trust the person or the group or the organization to use your gift properly, you ought to give it somewhere else—to something and to someone whom you will trust to use it as it is supposed to be used. The apostles distributed the goods.

> Verses 36 and 37:
> And Joses, who by the apostles was surnamed Barnabas, (which is, being interpreted, The son of consolation,) a Levite, *and* of the country of Cyprus,
>
> Having land [singular], sold *it,* and brought the money, and laid *it* at the apostles' feet.

We just read that the early Christians sold only their plurality. Yet, here is a man who sold his land, a singular possession. Why? He was a Levite. According to the Old Testament a Levite should not own any property. Joses, whose name was Barnabas from Cyprus, understanding and believing the teaching, was converted and saved. Therefore he sold his singular property which he should never have owned, and he brought the money therefrom and laid it at the apostles' feet.

Now we have in a nutshell some idea of how the first-century Church operated and, thereby, prospered so that many were won to the Lord Jesus Christ and manifested God's power. Time and again we see these principles:

1. Each person was responsible to witness with boldness about the Word of God and then stand by those newborn Christians until they could walk forth and, in turn, witness on their own.

2. The Church prospered when small groups (churches, fellowships) gathered in homes and ministered under the supervision of capable overseers.

3. Apostles, prophets, evangelists, pastors, and teachers kept in continual contact with each group by revisitations and written communications.

4. Christians contributed to the welfare of the Church and its members by giving to the common need, in contributing the plurality of their material possessions.

By reading Acts and the Pauline Epistles, one quickly notes the numerical growth and spiritual prosperity of the first-century Church. The twentieth-century Church obviously doesn't compare in its vitality. Thus we have everything to gain by following the early Church's example. God hasn't changed. And since we still have His power, we can surely adapt the techniques of the early Church and couple it with the power of God within each of us as Christians. We are the ones who must apply these principles and this power and the apostles' boldness to make the twentieth-century Church stronger and more vital than the Christian Church has ever been. This is our opportunity and challenge. Herein we must stand fast.

Chapter Thirteen

WHY DIVISION?

Somewhere in our thinking, many of us have erroneously embraced the idea that when God moves, peace and tranquillity prevail. This concept was succinctly stated in a radio broadcast when the minister explained it thusly:

> Frequently we are mixed up when it comes to defining a movement of God. We think that confusion of any sort indicates that the whole thing is of Satan. Nothing could be further from the truth. A move of God always upsets the equilibrium of established order. For a time it seems to bring chaos into orderly lives and churches. The smug, complacent, and self-satisfied are tremendously disturbed. It is quoted that "God is not a God of confusion but of peace." This is true, but only in the Church will this peace be found. In the world, as well as in the "merely professing" church, there is to be found confusion and every evil work. The move of

God upsets everything carnal, fleshly, self-ish, and devilish.

In the fourteenth chapter of Acts we are told of a movement of God. It took place in Iconium, and the evangelists were Paul and Barnabas. What happened was not just an isolated instance; such events seemed to have been much the pattern wherever Paul and Barnabas preached. Arriving at Iconium from Antioch in Pisidia, they witnessed the same sort of confusion as had transpired elsewhere.

Acts 14:1:
And it came to pass in Iconium, that they went both together into the synagogue of the Jews [Judeans], and so spake, that a great multitude both of the Jews [Judeans] and also of the Greeks believed.

There was a mighty turning to God among the Judeans and the Gentiles; but all was not sweetness and light.

Verse 2:
But the unbelieving Jews [Judeans] stirred up the Gentiles, and made their minds evil affected against the brethren.

Did the attitude of the unbelievers stop Paul and Barnabas from ministering? Not at all.

Verse 3:
Long time therefore abode they speaking boldly in the Lord, which gave testimony unto the word of his grace, and granted signs and wonders to be done by their hands.

How could they cease preaching when God continued to do great signs and wonders under their ministry? But despite these marvels of grace, there were those who would not believe.

Verse 4:
But the multitude of the city was divided: and part held with the Jews [Judeans], and part with the apostles.

Here was division and confusion. Not just a home or a church was divided, but an entire city. The tension did not subside, but rather became worse.

Verse 5:
...there was an assault made both of the Gentiles, and also of the Jews [Judeans] with their rulers, to use *them* despitefully, and to stone them.

189

Here was riot and violence. Some people will say, "Surely if this was of God, all of this would not have happened." Yet this is what did happen and still does happen when truth is taught. The powers of darkness, even though religiously garbed, will fight. There must always be an exposure and destruction of evil whenever and wherever spiritual revival comes about.

Not the trouble, but the signs and wonders that accompanied Paul and Barnabas testified to the fact that God had called them, and that they indeed brought about the move of God. Signs follow those sent by the Lord. They speak with new tongues. They cast out devils in the name of Jesus Christ. When men of God lay hands upon the sick, they arise whole, for with God there "is no variableness." He answers needs constantly.

These saints of God, Paul and Barnabas, barely escaped with their lives from Iconium, but they moved on into Lystra and Derbe. In Lystra the people wanted to make gods of Paul and Barnabas, and the priest of Jupiter could hardly be restrained from offering sacrifices to them. But Paul and his companion would have none of this activity. They intervened among these idolaters and succeeded in halting the entire proceeding. As a matter of fact, Paul and Barnabas were so successful that the tide changed against them, and in a short time the people attacked and stoned Paul and dragged him out of the city, supposing him to be dead.

The number of us who would like to have a part in such a movement as this is probably infinitesimal, and yet this was a movement of God. Experiences of this sort could be related by the score, both in apostolic days and ever since.

The Lollards, who were organized by Wycliffe in the fourteenth century, were instructed "to go about and preach to the poor in their own tongue, working in harmony with the clergy if they would allow them, but against them or independent of them if they were hostile."

The leaders of the spiritual movements in the Church have always been ridiculed and maligned. The confusing element in the entire situation is that it is the religious people, those who are deeply sincere, who cause the division. The world appears to evince little initial interest regarding a movement of God and pays virtually no attention. As Acts 7 points out, it is the religious element who are the persecutors and resisters.

> Acts 7:51 and 52:
>
> Ye stiffnecked and uncircumcised in heart and ears, ye do always resist the Holy Ghost: as your fathers *did,* so *do* ye.
>
> Which of the prophets have not your fathers persecuted? and they have slain them which shewed before of the coming of the Just One; of whom ye have been now the betrayers and murderers.

The Pharisees would not accept Jesus as the Christ. The Judeans stirred up the multitude against Paul and Barnabas. The religious people of the day stoned Stephen. Division always frustrates Christian efforts.

May God deliver us as the Church from being contentious and difficult, from maligning our brethren, from bickering and quarrelsomeness, from dividing the Body of Christ by our lack of enlightenment. There is too much division outside the Church; our solidarity is imperative to give us strength to move forward in spite of the opposition. May the Father in heaven, for the sake of the only begotten Son, bless us with such an abundance that we may cease to be a part of the problem and become a part of the answer. May we as members of Christ's Body become so filled with love that we may be teachable and have our hearts opened to God's Holy Word. And may we receive of Him and carry the blessing to all we meet, that they may see us and know we are His.

PART V

LIVING THE WORD

PART V

LIVING THE WORD

In a step-by-step manner the overall structure of this book builds knowledge relating to the new, dynamic Church, the Church of the Body. After establishing the difference between the Church of the Bride and the Church of the Body, we studied God's plan for us as members of the Body of Christ.

As God's children, God put in us His investment of eternal life and the manifestations of the holy spirit. All of this latent power we received when we confessed Jesus as lord of our lives and believed that God raised him from the dead. "A Christian's Power Base" showed how to activate that latent power and manifest God's presence and power in the world of the senses.

After understanding the relationship of God and each of His sons as individuals, we briefly looked at His sons acting collectively as the Church. Certain patterns of organization and behavior were established by the dynamic early Church which we can apply to the called-out of our times and get effective results for the twentieth-century Church.

The culmination of all our knowledge of God's Word comes with our day-by-day living as mature Christians. To walk in fellowship with the power God gave to us, we must study and know God's message for His sons during the Age of Grace. The final part of "Living the Word" is an enlightening study of several chapters from the Epistles. These studies, "The High Calling," "The Christian's Joy and Crown," and "The Answer," give us knowledge, encouragement, correction, and all things necessary to live the type of life which God wants for and expects of His sons who make up the Church of the Body, the new, dynamic Church.

Chapter Fourteen

THE HIGH CALLING
A STUDY OF PHILIPPIANS 3

In the first verse of Philippians 3, Paul by revelation says, "Finally, my brethren, rejoice in the Lord...." A person cannot rejoice until he has first experienced joy. Rejoicing is a repeat performance of joy. We rejoice in the Lord; if we rejoice in anything or anyone else, we are going to be let down.

> Philippians 3:1:
> Finally, my brethren, rejoice in the Lord. To write the same things to you, to me indeed *is* not grievous [irksome], but for you *it is* safe [gives certainty, reinforces].

What "same things"? The things he had already told them through his helper Epaphroditus.

Verse 2:
Beware of dogs,* beware of evil workers
[those with evil intent], beware of the concision.

"Concision" is an interesting word in this particular instance referring to the mutilation of
physical bodies. Christ was the end of the law,
but legalistic believers continued to teach that
one who believed in Christ had to be circum-
cised in order to be a Christian, even as things
are taught today, perhaps having substituted other
legalistic practices.

Verse 3:
For we are the circumcision, which worship
God in the spirit, and rejoice in Christ Jesus,
and have no confidence in the flesh.

We who worship God in spirit are the circumcision. The literal translation according to
the critical Greek texts and Aramaic Peshitta text
is: "We are the circumcision who worship by
the spirit of God" or "...who worship God via
the spirit."

---

*"Dogs" is the figure of speech called *hypocatastasis*. Its
usage here means "backbiters."

To "worship God in the spirit" does not mean to worship by contributing to the collection plate. There is only one way we can worship God "in spirit," and that is by speaking in tongues. To worship in the spirit, a person must have spirit; all other ritual is part of the senses realm. We cannot worship God by the senses, for He "dwelleth not in temples made with hands."* As John 4:24 pointedly declares, "God *is* a Spirit: and they that worship him must worship *him* in spirit and in truth." To worship Him in spirit can only be by speaking in tongues. If the Word means what it says and says what it means, then these truths are fabulous. The Word *always* causes us to joy and rejoice.

The last part of Philippians 3:3 says, "and rejoice in Christ Jesus, and have no confidence in the flesh." "The flesh" refers to body and soul. Those of us who are born again of the Spirit of God have a third part—spirit. The spirit should be the foremost interest in our total being.

We are the circumcision, the chosen, who worship by way of the spirit. We can *rejoice* in Christ Jesus because we at one time experienced

---

*Acts 17:24: "God that made the world and all things therein, seeing that he is Lord of heaven and earth, dwelleth not in temples made with hands."

joy in Christ Jesus. Rejoicing in Christ Jesus is only possible by renewing the mind and focusing on spiritual matters—trusting in things spiritual rather than trusting or having confidence in the flesh. We do not go by what the senses promote; we abide in the Word and the revelation of the spirit.

> Verses 4-7:
> Though I might also have confidence in the flesh. If any other man thinketh that he hath whereof he might trust in the flesh, I more:
>
> Circumcised the eighth day, of the stock of Israel, *of* the tribe of Benjamin, an Hebrew of the Hebrews; as touching the law, a Pharisee;
>
> Concerning zeal, persecuting the church; touching the righteousness which is in the law, blameless.
>
> But what things were gain to me, those I counted [declared] loss for Christ.

What things were personal gain to Paul? He just listed seven personal gains in verses five and six.

Verse 8:
Yea doubtless, and I count all things *but* loss for the excellency of the knowledge of Christ Jesus my Lord: for whom I have suffered the loss of all things, and do count them *but* dung, that I may win [gain] Christ.

Paul considered all his previous academic training and social and religious positions but excretion in comparison to "the knowledge of Christ Jesus my Lord...that I may win Christ."

Verse 9:
And be found in him, not having mine own righteousness, which is of the law, but that which is through the faith of Christ, the righteousness which is of God by faith.

If righteousness were achieved by one's own efforts and good behavior, then a person could not glory in Christ. The glory would belong to himself. But righteousness is not achieved by works or by keeping the law. Righteousness is through, or by way of, the faith of Jesus Christ unto all and upon all who believe.*

---

*Romans 3:22: "Even the righteousness of God *which is* by faith of Jesus Christ unto all and upon all them that believe: for there is no difference."

Verse 10:
That I may know him, and the power of his resurrection, and the fellowship of his sufferings, being made conformable unto his death.

The word "know" means "to know by personal spiritual experience," which is possible only to those who are righteous. "That I may know him experientially as my savior and the inherent power [the *dunamis*] of his resurrection."

"And the fellowship" refers to baptism into Christ Jesus. This means that we were buried with him, and raised up from the dead, now to walk completely in this new life. Legally when he died, we died with him; when he was buried, we were buried with him; when he arose, we arose with him.* Being with him in "the fellowship of his sufferings" we were "made conformable [like he was] unto his death."

"That I may know him [experientially as my savior], and the [inherent] power [the *dunamis*] of his resurrection, and the fellowship [of his

---

*Colossians 2:12: "Buried with him in baptism, wherein also ye are risen with *him* through the faith of the operation of God, who hath raised him from the dead."

death, burial, resurrection] of his sufferings, being [therefore, we are] made conformable [like he was] unto his death."

Verse 11:
If by any means I might attain [come] unto the resurrection of the dead.

"Unto" is the Greek word *eis,* which is always used with the accusative case. In mathematics this word *eis,* "unto" of verse 11, is the movement toward an object with the intent of reaching the object. That is its literal usage. "If by any means I might come toward the objective with the intent of reaching it."

The word translated "resurrection" is the Greek word *exanastasis,* which means "out resurrection." Here Paul is not concerned with the resurrections of the just and the unjust as noted in Revelation 20:5 and 13; he is concerned with an "out resurrection." The "out resurrection" is spoken of in I Thessalonians 4:16 and 17: "...the dead in Christ shall rise first: Then we which are alive *and* remain shall be caught up...." Paul did not care to die; he wanted to be changed through the "out resurrection." This "out resurrection" or *exanastasis* should literally be translated "out from among." "If by any means I might reach out toward the coming of the lord."

> Philippians 3:12:
> Not as though I had already attained [Paul had not arrived at that "out resurrection" yet.], either were already perfect: but I follow after, if that I may apprehend [attain to] that for which also I am [was] apprehended [attained] of [by] Christ Jesus.

He was appointed by Christ Jesus to live this life, to carry out the ministry, to believe, to know that he was crucified with him, to know that he arose with him.

> Verse 13:
> Brethren, I count not myself to have apprehended [attained]: but *this* one thing *I do,* forgetting those things which are behind, and reaching forth unto those things which are before.

Paul says that he is forgetting his ancestry: Hebrew of the Hebrews, his education at the feet of Gamaliel, and other reasons for earthly acclaim. Paul now is reaching for those things

which are ahead. If we would only do this—
forget about the past—we would profit.

Verse 14:
I press ["follow after," as in verse 12] toward
the mark [finish line] for the prize of the
high calling of God in Christ Jesus.

In a race or in a track meet, the finish line
determines the winner. Paul says he will press
toward the finish line which will culminate in
the prize of the high calling of God in Christ
Jesus.

Verse 15:
Let us therefore, as many as be perfect, be
thus minded: and if in any thing ye be otherwise minded, God shall reveal even this
unto you.

The word "perfect" means "initiated ones,"
those who have been brought into the inner
secrets of the great mystery, that Mystery which
was kept secret from the foundation of the world
and was first made manifest unto the Apostle
Paul as recorded in Ephesians 3:3. Paul here is
talking to those who know that Mystery, the initiated ones, those who have gone further with
the Lord than just being pledges or neophytes

or carnal Christians. "Let us therefore, as many as be perfect [initiated], be thus minded..."—be intent on reaching the finish line. "...And if in any thing ye be otherwise minded,"—if you have any other goal—"God shall reveal even this unto you" by a continued accurate study and right dividing of the Word or by revelation.

> Philippians 3:16-18:
> Nevertheless, whereto we have already attained, let us [all] walk by the same rule, let us mind the same thing [with the same minds].
>
> Brethren, be followers together of me, and mark them which walk so as ye have us for an ensample [example].
>
> (For many walk, of whom I have told you often, and now tell you [again] even [with] weeping, *that* [those people who so walk] *they are* the enemies of the cross of Christ.

Brothers in Christ should be examples, not counterfeits. The people in verse 18 looked sincere and religious, yet the Word says they were the enemies of the cross of Christ because they were not walking according to the revealed Word, with the same mind.

Verse 19:
Whose end *is* destruction, whose God *is*
their belly, and *whose* glory *is* in their
shame, who mind earthly things.)

"Whose end *is* destruction, whose God *is their*
belly...." The word "belly" is the figure of
speech called a *synecdoche,* meaning that one
part or member represents the whole. The enemies of the cross are their own god, "*whose*
glory *is* in their shame, who mind earthly things."
Earthly things are fleshly things, things of the
senses. They are obedient to things of the senses;
they have confidence in the flesh rather than in
the things of the Word of God.

Verse 20:
For our conversation [citizenship, *politeuma*]
is in heaven; from whence also we look for
the Saviour, the Lord Jesus Christ.

Do we pray that the lord may return? No, we
just look for the savior; we cannot influence his
return. Man had nothing to do with Christ's first
coming, for the Bible says in Galatians 4:4,
"...when the fulness of the time was come, God
sent forth his [only begotten] Son...." Likewise,
when the fullness of time comes again, Acts 1:11

reveals that "...this same Jesus, which is taken up from you into heaven, shall so come in like manner as ye have seen him go...." All we do is look with expectation for this "out resurrection." "...We look for the Saviour, [who is] the Lord Jesus Christ."

What about the teaching that we are to build the Kingdom of God upon earth, that we are to bring Utopia to this world? The Bible tells that the earth is going to become progressively worse. The only one who is ever going to get the world out of the turmoil which man has made of it is the Lord Jesus Christ. We must focus our undivided attention upon the Lord Jesus Christ, looking for him.

> Philippians 3:21:
> Who shall change our vile body, that it may be fashioned like unto his glorious body, according to the working [ability] whereby he is able even to subdue all things unto himself.

Our physical bodies have the nature of death written into them; that is why Philippians 3:21 calls them "vile." Our death-prone bodies will "be fashioned like unto his glorious body." Who will change our bodies "like unto his glorious

210

body"? The Lord Jesus Christ will "according to the working whereby he is able even to subdue all things unto himself." When we have a body fashioned like unto his glorious body, we will then know even as we are now known. In the meantime, we joy and rejoice in him because we have the certainty of his presence and power within.

Chapter Fifteen

THE CHRISTIAN'S JOY
AND CROWN
A STUDY OF PHILIPPIANS 4

Philippians 4:1:
Therefore, my brethren dearly beloved and longed for, my joy and crown, so stand fast in the Lord, *my* dearly beloved.

The first word in Philippians 4 indicates that something has gone before. "Therefore" is a conjunction, and in order to understand what "therefore" concludes, we must turn back two verses.

Philippians 3:20 and 21:
For our conversation [*politeuma,* citizenship] is in heaven; from whence also we look for the Saviour, the Lord Jesus Christ:

Who shall change our vile body, that it may be fashioned like unto his glorious body, according to the working whereby he is able even to subdue all things unto himself.

As Christians, our citizenship is in heaven, and we can look forward to Christ's return when our bodies will be like his resurrected body and when Christ will subdue all things—*therefore,* because of this knowledge, we, "dearly beloved and longed for, my joy and crown, so stand fast in the Lord, *my* dearly beloved." Men and women should want to stand fast in the Lord because of what Christ has done for them and because he is coming back.

According to the first verse of Philippians 4, who are the joy and crown of the Apostle Paul? The ones to whom he taught the Word of God. To those saved under his ministry Paul said, "You are my joy and crown; you stand fast." Twice he refers to those whom he has taught as "dearly beloved." Clearly, Paul has a strong attachment to these people.

In I Thessalonians Paul again points out that his brothers in Christ—those who had become brothers because of his ministry—were his joy and crown.

I Thessalonians 2:19 and 20:
For what *is* our hope, or joy, or crown of rejoicing? *Are* not even ye in the presence of our Lord Jesus Christ at his coming?

For ye are our glory and joy.

With the coming of the Lord Jesus Christ, those whom Paul had taught, those who were his hope, joy, and crown, will appear before the Father, "...even ye in the presence of our Lord Jesus Christ at his coming."

The words "stand fast" used in Philippians 4:1 in the phrase "so stand fast in the Lord, *my* dearly beloved" are the same usage as in Philippians 1:27: "...that ye stand fast in one spirit, with one mind striving together for the faith [family faith]* of the gospel."

"Stand fast" literally means "to remain strong." When we stand together, we are strong. If I am strong in the Lord and you are strong in the Lord, together we move ahead. The ministry of the Apostle Paul as recorded in Acts 19 is an example of people who were strong in the Lord

---

*The "common" faith of Titus 1:4 and the "household" of faith in Galatians 6:10 make up the "family" faith because Christianity is a family affair: the Father with His family, His children. God is our Father; we are His children.

and, thus, they bore fruit. Acts 19 says that Paul took those strong in the faith and discussed the Word of God at the school of Tyrannus. Two years later *all* Asia Minor had heard of the Lord Jesus.

It was simply miraculous how the Word of God was spread throughout the country. Yet, notice that II Timothy 1:15 records that all Asia forsook Paul. Paul's "joy and crown" apparently did not "stand fast" very long and thus their spiritual muscles became flaccid. The "joy and crown" became so weak that even before Paul died, the greatness of the revelation which God had given to him had already been lost. And, for the most part, this knowledge is still lost today; very few people know about the Mystery of "Christ in you, the hope of glory."*

The Word says that all Asia heard the Word of the Lord Jesus; yet later, all Asia had left Paul. This reminds one of the Lord Jesus Christ, who had the multitudes following him because of signs, miracles, and wonders. However, when the time approached for him to be crucified, all fled and the rabble cried, "Crucify him! Crucify him!"

---

*Colossians 1:27: "To whom God would make known what *is* the riches of the glory of this mystery among the Gentiles; which is Christ in you, the hope of glory."

Only when we as believers stand fast in the Lord will we be witnesses to the greatness of the Word.

> Philippians 4:2:
> I beseech [implore] Euodias, and beseech Syntyche, that they be of the same mind in the Lord.

Paul said, "I implore you two to be of the same mind in the Lord." These two believers disagreed. They were of different minds; therefore, they could not be strong in the Lord. If we are strong in the Lord we cannot have two opinions regarding truth. There can be two opinions regarding facts, but not regarding truth. The moment we begin having an opinion about truth, we are already wrong. Truth is truth; it is "thus saith the Lord." What we think does not make any difference. The reason we have opinions is that we do not "rightly divide"* the Word. If the Word of God is rightly divided, we have the true Word; when it is wrongly divided, we have error. When we wrongly divide the Word we are working for Satan. Whenever the Word is rightly divided, it again means, "Thus saith the Lord."

---

*II Timothy 2:15: "Study to shew thyself approved unto God, a workman that needeth not to be ashamed, rightly dividing the word of truth."

217

Paul implored Euodias and Syntyche, saying, "If you want to stand fast in the Lord, you must be of the same mind." One cannot be pulling one way and another the other way and expect to be strong in the Lord. Philippians 2:2 corroborates the truth that strength comes with being of one accord: "Fulfil ye my joy, that ye be likeminded, having the same love, *being* of one accord, of one mind." Paul's joy was fulfilled when they walked in the same mind. To have the same mind is to be of one accord, to have unity of purpose.

> Philippians 4:3:
> And I intreat thee also, true yokefellow, help those women which laboured with me in the gospel, with Clement also, and *with* other my fellowlabourers, whose names *are* in the book of life.

This is the only place in the Bible where the word "yokefellow" is used. Women also worked with the Apostle Paul in spreading the gospel. Why, then, should people say that women have no right to preach, teach, or share the Word?

When the Word says "whose names *are* in the book of life," the book of life means a living, spiritual record of events which belongs to God.

This is not a literal book, but rather a figure of speech. Our parents did not need a paper book to write down our names in order to know that we belonged to them; neither do we need a book to keep a record of our children's names and works. Just living is the record. So also are we in the mind of God. The Word says that He knew us from before the foundation of the world. God knew who would believe on His Son and would therefore be part of His family.

Verse 4:
Rejoice in the Lord alway: *and* again I say, Rejoice.

If we know what we have in Christ, then we should rejoice in him.

Verse 5:
Let your moderation [forbearance or pa- tience or self-control] be known unto all men. The Lord *is* at hand.

The word "known" is a very unique word. There are five different Greek words for "to know"; it is the little differences of meaning that illuminate the accuracy of the Word. "Known" here is "to know by having learned or expe- rienced."

"Let your moderation be known unto all men" does not fit into the Word. Why should our moderation be known to all men? It should be nobody else's business. No man should be judged in meat, in drink, or in respect of an holy day. No man is to be our judge. When these words are accurately understood, the verse literally says, "Learn by experience forbearance toward all men."

"The Lord *is* at hand" means "the lord is *always* at hand." This statement has nothing to do with the second coming. It simply exhorts the believers by reminding us that we have Christ in us. He is watching over us, so let us be mindful of this. Verse 5 says, "Learn by experience forbearance toward all men, for Christ is in us."

> Verse 6:
> Be careful for nothing; but in every thing by prayer and supplication with thanksgiving let your requests [special petitions] be made known [declared] unto God.

Verse 6 begins with the clause, "Be careful for nothing." These words do not fit into the Word in the way a modern reader understands them. The word "careful" means "anxious." The statement literally means, "Do not be filled with anxiety regarding anything." We should be careful when it comes to the Word of God, but not worried and anxious because Christ is in us.

The key to "prayer and supplication" is in being specific regarding one's need and want. "Specifically, let your needs be declared unto God with thanksgiving," that your mind may be renewed in what you have in Him.

> Verse 7:
> And the peace of God, which passeth all understanding, shall [absolutely] keep your hearts and minds [thoughts] through [in] Christ Jesus.

When we declare our requests with thanksgiving, the peace of God, which passes all understanding, shall keep our hearts and thoughts in Christ Jesus. Isn't this a wonderful verse? There are two points made in this verse: one is salvation and the other is fellowship. The "peace of God, which passeth all understanding, shall [absolutely] keep your hearts...." The seat of your spiritual life remains in God's keeping because it is seed; this is eternal life. Therefore, because this is true, we keep our thoughts in Christ Jesus and we are of one mind walking according to the Word of God. Paul says, "Then you are my joy, my crown."

221

Verse 8:
Finally, brethren, whatsoever things are true,
whatsoever things *are* honest, whatsoever
things *are* just, whatsoever things *are* pure,
whatsoever things *are* lovely, whatsoever
things *are* of good report; if *there be* any
virtue, and if *there be* any praise, think on
these things.

Think! What we mentally dwell on we are
going to manifest. We never rise beyond what
we think. The Word of God says that our thoughts
are to be in Christ Jesus. If our thoughts are in
Christ Jesus, then we think that which is true,
honest, just, pure, lovely, and of good report. It
is just as easy to think good as it is to think
evil except that the influence of our society is
so negative that we must purposefully work to
keep our thoughts positive. We must willfully
determine whether we are going to think as the
Word says or think as the world does.

Verses 9-11:
Those things, which ye have both learned,
and received, and heard, and seen in me,
[you] do: and [if you do] the God of peace
shall be with you.

But I rejoiced in the Lord greatly, that now
at the last your care [thinking] of me hath

flourished again; wherein ye were also careful [mindful], but ye lacked opportunity.

Not that I speak in respect of want: for I have learned, in whatsoever state I am, *therewith* to be content.

Paul said he was not complaining about his needs, for he had learned that in whatever state he was, to be self-adequate, not "content" as the KJV says. The text literally reads: "I learned in whatsoever state I am, I am self-adequate." "Christ in you" makes you self-adequate. Are you lacking anything according to the Word of God? The Word says, "...ye are complete in him...."* If we are complete, we are complete; we cannot lack anything. Therefore, in every situation we are more than conquerors; we are self-sufficient because we are complete in him.

Verse 12:
I know both how to be abased, and I know how to abound: every where and in all things I am instructed both to be full and to be hungry, both to abound and to suffer need.

---

*Colossians 2:10: "And ye are complete in him, which is the head of all principality and power."

223

When Paul had little, he was still self-adequate. "...I am instructed both to be full and to be hungry, both to abound and to suffer need."

The meaning of "instructed" in the text is "to be initiated into the secret," the secret being how to be self-sufficient, or self-adequate, whether we lack or whether we have abundance—"feast or famine." Paul had been "initiated into the secret" of how to live.

Because some have never been initiated into the secret, they stay in poverty. If they ever had an abundance, they wouldn't know what to do with it. We might paraphrase Paul's statement thus: "I have been initiated into the secret. When it comes to having physical or material needs, I move on; when I abound in material and physical possessions, I move on also. In every situation, I am self-adequate."

Verse 13:
I can do all things through Christ which strengtheneth me.

Paul was talking about how to live with an abundance and how to live on a shoestring; in either situation we are self-adequate. Why are we self-adequate? Because we have strength through Christ who strengthens us.

Many people use this scripture in regard to giving up chewing tobacco, smoking, and other nonbeneficial habits. This verse does not relate at all to such things. It deals specifically with having or not having a sufficiency in material matters.

Verse 14:
Notwithstanding ye have well done, that ye did communicate with my affliction.

In other words, "Ye have well done, having had fellowship with my affliction." Most people believe that "affliction" means "sickness." The word "affliction" is explained in the last word of verse 16, "necessity." Paul said, "Ye have well done, having had fellowship with my necessity." This verse is most easily understood if we ourselves have been in the same situation. If we have always had an abundance of material things and never suffered need, we have not experienced "the fellowship of necessities." Paul was saying that the believers in Philippi understood because they themselves had at one time suffered lack and at another time known abundance.

Verses 15-17:
Now ye Philippians know also, that in the

beginning of the gospel, when I departed
from Macedonia, no church communicated
with me as concerning giving and receiving, but ye only.

For even in Thessalonica ye sent once and
again [twice] unto my necessity.

Not because I desire [seek] a gift: but I
desire fruit that may abound to your account.

Paul was not seeking a gift from the
Philippians because he did not ask them for material things; but Paul desired that fruit might
abound to their account. Every time these people communicated with the necessity of the
Apostle Paul, each time they gave to his material needs, God set the good works to their
account.

Verse 18:
But I have all, and abound: I am full, having
received of Epaphroditus the things *which
were sent* from you, an odour of a sweet
smell, a sacrifice acceptable, wellpleasing to
God.

All they did was to communicate with the
necessity of the Apostle Paul, and Paul taught

that this was well pleasing and acceptable to God, and was set to their account. Their generous actions had nothing to do with their salvation; good works were simply credits to their walk and reward.

Verse 19:
But my God shall supply all your need according to his riches in glory by Christ Jesus.

In context you will understand this verse. "God shall supply all your need" literally refers to material things, not to spiritual things. The Philippians had given of their material things to the Apostle Paul; they ministered to his necessity. Paul is saying, "Now that you have communicated toward me, God will now supply all *your* need according to His riches in glory by Christ Jesus." Again we see the law at work: give and receive. This law works with reliability. God shall supply your material needs "according to his riches in glory by Christ Jesus." By His foreknowledge He knows our need before we ask.

Verses 20 and 21:
Now unto God and our Father *be* glory [our knowledge of Him] for ever and ever. Amen.

> Salute every saint in Christ Jesus. The brethren which are with me greet you.

Verse 21 admonishes us to greet every believer in *Christ Jesus*. The Word never says a believer is in Jesus. That would not be accurate, because the name "Jesus" is always associated with his humility. Whenever people wanted to humiliate him, they called him "Jesus." Even the devil spirits never called him "Christ" in the Word; they always said "Jesus." The name "Christ" means "anointed" or "anointing." In John 1:41 is the same word, "Messias, which is, being interpreted, the Christ [the promised, anointed one]." According to Acts 2:36, "God hath made that same Jesus [the humiliated one]... both Lord and Christ." According to Acts 10:38, "God anointed Jesus of Nazareth with the Holy Ghost...." This anointing made Jesus the Christ: the promised, anointed one (*Messiah*) to Israel. We are in *Christ Jesus* and not in *Jesus*.

> Philippians 4:22:
> All the saints salute you, chiefly [especially] they that are of Caesar's household.

It is interesting to note the Word of God at least touched the high government circles in the early days. Here we are told that the gospel had reached into Caesar's household.

Verse 23:
The grace of our Lord Jesus Christ *be* with you all. Amen.

We as Christians should "stand fast in the Lord" in our day-by-day walks, for as we walk we have the joy and peace found in the "one mind," and we have the physical and material blessings needed for the more abundant life now. We do have "all sufficiency for all things," and as sons of God we are in every situation self-adequate. The grace of our Lord Jesus Christ is with each of us. Amen.

Chapter Sixteen

THE ANSWER

A STUDY OF I JOHN

The Church of Grace was founded on the day of Pentecost, and with its founding began a new administration. John addressed his first epistle to those newly born into the fellowship to inform them of their position, rights, and responsibilities in the sight of God. When the words "from the beginning" are used in the first verse, it does not refer to the "in the beginning" as in Genesis 1:1. "The beginning" is found in seven verses in this epistle; in six it refers to the beginning of this administration, the period of the Church of Grace; once it refers to the time of beginning when iniquity was found in the Devil.

I John 1:1:
That which was from the beginning, which we have heard, which we have seen with our eyes, which we have looked upon, and our hands have handled, of the Word of life.

Hearing, seeing, and handling are in the realm of the five senses. The Word can be known to the natural man through his five senses—he has no other way by which to become knowledgeable.

> Verse 2:
> (For the life was manifested, and we have seen *it,* and bear witness, and shew unto you that eternal life, which was with the Father, and was manifested unto us.)

John is informing the people that he is going to make known his revelation concerning this "Word of life."

> Verse 3:
> That which we have seen and heard declare we unto you, that ye also may have fellowship with us: and truly our fellowship *is* with the Father, and with his Son Jesus Christ.

A child cannot have fellowship in an earthly family until after his birth. This is true of God's spiritual family also. We must be born again of God before we can have fellowship with God in His family. John is writing not to the unbelievers but to those who are sons, to those who are born again, so that they may have fellowship with God and with the other believers.

Verse 4:
And these things write we unto you, that your joy may be full.

Joy is also a fruit of the spirit as mentioned in Galatians 5:22 where it says, "But the fruit of the Spirit is... joy...." The fruit of the spirit does not include happiness. A man may have happiness from the material things around him; an abundance of things may make him happy. But joy is an *inside* job. Joy is a spiritual quality. The revelation in I John is written that the born-again believer may not only have joy within, but that his renewed-mind joy may be full.

I John 1:5:
This then is the message which we have heard of him, and declare unto you, that God is light, and in him is no darkness at all.

If God is Light, then there can be no darkness in Him. Everything negative, evil, harmful, sinful, and death-provoking must be from a source other than the true God of light.

233

Verse 6:
If we say that we have fellowship with him, and walk in darkness, we lie, and do not the truth.

After a person is a son in the household of God, he can have fellowship in the family as he follows the Word as his guidebook. If we as sons say that we have fellowship with God and yet do not follow the rule book and walk ungodly, we lie. When we stray outside the guidelines, we are out of fellowship, yet we remain sons in the household. We must clearly note the difference between fellowship and sonship. To "walk in darkness" does not break the Father-son relationship; it breaks the fellowship.

Verse 7:
But if we walk in the light, as he [God] is in the light, we have fellowship one with another, and the blood of Jesus Christ his Son cleanseth us from all sin.

Walking in the light gives us fellowship with God. When we are out of fellowship, we walk in darkness, which is sin, since all broken fellowship is sin. However, when we confess our broken fellowship, the blood of Jesus Christ cleanses us, makes us without blemish. "The blood" is a figure of speech referring to Jesus Christ's giving his life. It is the figure *metalepsis* which includes *synecdoche*. "Blood" is put by the figure *synecdoche* for "blood-shedding" indicating the death of Jesus Christ as distinct from his life. Then it goes beyond his death as an act, indicating the merits he accomplished for us which he effected by his death and are thus logically associated with it. The word "cleanseth" denotes cleansing through and through, leaving no imperfection or impurity.

Verses 8-10:
If we say that we have no sin [broken fellowship], we deceive ourselves, and the truth is not in us.

If we confess our sins [broken fellowship], he [God] is faithful and just to forgive us *our* sins [broken fellowship], and to cleanse us from all unrighteousness.

If we say that we have not sinned [broken fellowship], we make him [God] a liar, and his [God's] word is not in us [in our minds].

No man can live in fellowship with God if he lives according to any other principles than those of God's Word. When we walk in other paths, we sin, which is unrighteousness. If, when we are out of fellowship, we confess our sins to God, God is true to His promise to provide legal justice. God is able to absolve us of all broken fellowship, a sin of which all sons are guilty.

> I John 2:1 and 2:
> My little children, these things write I unto you, that ye sin not [that you do not break fellowship]. And [but] if any man sin [breaks fellowship], we have an advocate [a defense attorney] with the Father, Jesus Christ the righteous:
>
> And he [Jesus Christ] is the propitiation [payment] for our sins [broken fellowship]: and not for ours only, but also for *the sins of* the whole world.

Jesus Christ is the propitiation for our sins, meaning that he not only paid for them but he also wins us back into favor with God when we break fellowship. Our confession of sin brings forgiveness of our broken fellowship. God can remit our sin only once, and that is at the time of salvation. Remission of sins is for the unsaved sinner; forgiveness of sin is for the saved sinner who is out of fellowship with God.

Verse 3:
And hereby we do know that we know him [God], if we keep his [God's] commandments.

We are to prove to ourselves that we know God. The two Greek forms for "know" in verse 3 are used with precision as follows: "We do know [present tense—by being well acquainted personally] that we know [perfect tense—by an initial meeting, salvation, with God]...." What are His commandments? To do those things which He has just instructed—to walk in the light. We are to hold forth the Word after our minds have been illuminated by it.

Verse 4:
He [the man] that saith, I know [by a personal acquaintance] him [God], and keepeth not his commandments, is a liar, and the truth is not in him [the man].

If a person is not born again, the truth is not in him spiritually. But if a born-again believer says that he knows God intimately and does not observe the commandment to walk in the light, the truth of the Word is not in that man's mind. The truth remains in the believer's spiritual being, but that person has not put on the truth in his mind.

> Verse 5:
> But whoso keepeth his [God's] word, in him [the man] verily is the love of God perfected: hereby know we that we are in him [God by Jesus Christ].

To keep God's Word is to live according to His will. We do the keeping of His Word, and in the keeping of it, the love of God is perfected in us. Love, *agapē* in Greek, comes with spiritual birth. "Love [*agapē*] of God" is outwardly manifested when we walk in the light. Having the spirit from God in us plus walking in His love makes possible the perfect fellowship.

> Verse 6:
> He [the man] that saith he abideth in him [God by Christ Jesus] ought himself also so to walk, even as he [Jesus Christ] walked.

Anyone who says that he is abiding or continuing in the presence of God must have his mind renewed according to the Word and walk with this renewed mind as Jesus Christ did. The born-again believer can, because of freedom of will, choose to live according to this world; but to be in fellowship, a believer must choose to renew his mind and act according to the Word of God.

> Verses 7 and 8:
> Brethren, I write no new commandment unto you, but an old commandment which ye had from the beginning. The old commandment is the word which ye have heard from the beginning.
>
> Again, a new commandment I write unto you, which thing [entire transaction of word and deed] is true in him [God] and in you: because the darkness is past, and the true light now shineth.

A newly made precept is now given. The whole transaction of God was made genuine and applicable, and therefore is, and can be, manifested in the senses world. The darkness is past because God in Christ in us is light. This light cannot be seen by others, however, unless we manifest it, show it forth by our walk.

Verse 9:
He that saith he is in the light, and hateth his brother, is in darkness even until now.

Hate is possible only when someone is born of the seed of the Devil, just as *agapē* love is possible only when someone is born of God's seed. The two Greek words indicating "hate," *miseō* and *stugētos,* must be understood by their usage in the context. They may mean "dislike," or "dislike issuing in the absolute hate of the Devil." This hate, the opposite of *agapē,* is a spiritual quality brought into a person when he is born of the seed of the serpent.

Verses 10 and 11:
He [the man] that loveth his brother abideth in the light [walking in the renewed mind according to the Word], and there is none occasion of stumbling in him [the man].

But he that hateth [dislikes] his brother is in darkness, and walketh in darkness, and knoweth not whither he goeth, because that darkness hath blinded his eyes.

If we keep our minds renewed on God's Word, the love of God is perfected in our minds, and we give no opportunity to the flesh to dislike or slight a brother in Christ. He who slights or dislikes his brother has not renewed his mind on God's Word. Satan constantly tries to dissuade us from walking in the truth of the light and thus causes us to walk in darkness. In order to continue steadfast in the light, a believer must have a knowledge of God's Word. Without such knowledge, a believer is uprooted and is easily swayed into darkness because of ignorance.

Verse 12:
I write unto you, little children, because your sins are forgiven you for his [God's] name's sake.

A person cannot be a child of God until he is born again of God's seed. A man's sin, broken fellowship, is forgiven on account of God's name's sake, because the man is in God's family. Literally, all sins were laid on Jesus Christ when he made his sacrifice.

Verses 13 and 14:
I write unto you, fathers, because ye have known him *that is* from the beginning. I

write unto you, young men, because ye have overcome the wicked one [Satan]. I write unto you, little children, because ye have known the Father.

I have written unto you, fathers, because ye have known him [God] *that is* from the beginning. I have written unto you, young men, because ye are strong, and the word of God abideth in you, and ye have overcome the wicked one [Satan].

The Word of God can only dwell in men after they are born again and have eternal life. Believers abide in the Word as they renew their minds according to that Word. This is the only way to overcome the wicked one.

Verse 15:
Love not the world, neither the things *that are* in the world. If any man love the world, the love of the Father is not in him.

If the love of the Father is not in a person, that person does not have eternal life. If a man truly loves the things of the world (which refers to Satan, who rules and legally owns the world), the love of the Father cannot be in him.

Verse 16:
For all that *is* in the world, the lust of the
flesh, and the lust of the eyes, and the pride
of life, is not of the Father, but is of the
world.

Lust (desire for more than one needs), pos-
sessive desires ("lust of the eyes"), and boast-
ings ("pride") are all qualities of men in whom
the Word does not abide.

Verses 17 and 18:
And the world passeth away, and the lust
thereof: but he that doeth [practices] the will
of God abideth for ever.

Little children, it is the last time: and as ye
have heard that antichrist shall come, even
now are there many antichrists; whereby we
know that it is the last time.

Any person who is born of the seed of the
serpent is called "antichrist" because he is in
opposition to Christ.

Verse 19:
They went out from us, but they were not
of us; for if they had been of us, they would
no doubt have continued with us: but *they*

went out, that they might be made manifest that they were not all of us.

The antichrists, those born into the household of the Devil, wanted to separate themselves from the believers, those of the household of the true God.

Verses 20-24:
But ye have an unction from the Holy One, and ye know all things [because we have His written Word].

I have not written unto you because ye know not the truth, but because ye know it, and that no lie is of the truth.

Who is a liar but he that denieth that Jesus is the Christ? He is antichrist, that denieth the Father and the Son.

Whosoever denieth the Son, the same hath not the Father: *[but] he that acknowledgeth the Son hath the Father also.*

Let that therefore abide in you [in your mind], which ye have heard from the beginning. If that which ye have heard from the beginning shall remain in you [in your mind], ye also shall continue [to walk] in the Son, and in the Father.

244

If that which we have heard from the beginning, eternal life, is in us spiritually and we walk in fellowship by renewing our minds, we shall continue in the Father. Renewing our mind takes three steps: (1) know the Word of God, (2) put it into our mind, and (3) manifest it in actions. Salvation gives us sonship; the renewed mind gives us perfect fellowship with the Father.

> Verses 25-27:
> And this is the promise that he [God] hath promised us, *even* eternal life.
>
> These *things* have I written unto you concerning them that seduce you [cause you to doubt].
>
> But the anointing [the new birth] which ye have received of him abideth in you, and ye need not that any man teach you [instruct you]: but as the same anointing teacheth you of all things, and is truth, and is no lie, and even as it hath taught you, ye shall abide in him [God].

The anointing which we have from God is the anointing of holy spirit. It is receiving the fullness of the gift from the Holy Spirit Who is God. We need no man to teach us because we have the Word and the power and manifestations of the holy spirit.

245

Verse 28:
And now, little children, abide in him [in God through Christ Jesus]; that, when he [Christ] shall appear, we may have confidence [boldness], and not be ashamed before him [God] at his [Christ's] coming.

At the return of Christ, we are going to be judged and rewarded for our walk with God. If we live with the renewed mind in manifestation and are in fellowship with God, we will not be ashamed or feel dishonorable. Rather, we shall have confidence.

Verse 29:
If ye know that he [God] is righteous, ye know that every one that doeth righteousness is born of him [God].

"Doeth" is the key word. It means to practice a skill such as a professional surgeon, painter, or musician. We are to practice in the senses realm that which we have received in the spirit. We are righteous because God made us righteous; but our righteousness is manifested to the world as we practice the will of God, and the will of God is known only from the Word of God.

I John 3:1:
Behold, what manner of love the Father hath bestowed upon us, that we should be called the sons of God: therefore the world knoweth us not, because it knew him [God] not.

The world will never understand our being "sons of God." Salvation is an internal, spiritual working, and natural men cannot understand spiritual matters. The world does not know God, for as I Corinthians 2:14 explains, "...the natural man receiveth not the things of the Spirit of God: for they are foolishness unto him: neither can he know *them,* because they [spiritual matters] are spiritually discerned."

I John 3:2:
Beloved, now are we the sons of God, and [but] it doth not yet appear what we shall be: but we know that, when he [Christ] shall appear, we shall be like him; for we shall see him as he is.

Starting with the words "and it doth not yet appear" in verse 2 through verse 4 is a parenthetical section dealing with Christ. Then in verse 5 we return to the subject, God. To be like him (Christ) is to be as he will be in his resurrected body at his return. When Christ returns, we shall be like him because we are joint heirs with Christ* and sons of the same Father.

> Verse 3:
> And every man that hath this hope [Christ's return] in him purifieth himself, even as he [Christ] is pure.

We have hope for Christ's second coming. Thus, we who have this hope should purify ourselves by renewing the mind. Our minds should be made as pure by *us* as our spirits are pure, *the gift from God.*

> Verse 4:
> Whosoever committeth sin transgresseth also the law: for sin is the transgression of the law.

The phrase "transgression of the law" is the Greek word *anomia,* "lawlessness." One who practices illegalities, thereby not observing the

---

*Romans 8:17: "And if children, then heirs; heirs of God, and joint-heirs with Christ; if so be that we suffer with *him,* that we may be also glorified together."

law, is a transgressor. To fulfill the law, man must follow the instructions given in Galatians 6:2 where it says, "Bear ye one another's burdens, and so fulfil the law of Christ."

I John 3:5 and 6:
And ye know that he [God] was manifested [in Christ and shown to the world] to take away our sins; and in him [God] is no sin.

Whosoever abideth in him [God] sinneth not: whosoever sinneth hath not seen him [God], neither known [beyond initial acquaintance] him [God].

Verse 6 is speaking of a believer abiding in God (fellowship), *not* God abiding in a believer (salvation). A believer sins by breaking fellowship with God, not in the spiritual life which he received when he was born again, for that life is perfect and cannot sin. If one has a perfectly renewed mind, he does not sin because he does not break fellowship.

Verse 7:
Little children, let no man deceive you: he [the man] that doeth righteousness is righteous, even as he [God in Christ in you] is righteous.

No one can do righteousness until the person himself is righteous. Righteousness is of God and is therefore included in the gift, spirit. Righteousness is God in Christ within, which makes it possible to manifest righteousness without.

> Verse 8:
> He that committeth sin is of the devil; for the devil sinneth from the beginning. For this purpose the Son of God was manifested, that he [Jesus Christ] might destroy the works of the devil.

Every sin is due to the influence of Satan over the person committing the sin. Jesus Christ was manifested that he might break the power of Satan. In his first coming he did defeat the Devil's work; however, the total destruction is yet to take place with Christ's second coming.

The Son of God has defeated Satan for those who are born again and have renewed their minds according to the Word. If a person does not renew his mind, Satan is not defeated in that person's life. In such a case, Satan thwarts this person with diseases, worries, fears, and other satanic negatives.

The words "from the beginning" in verse 8 refer to the beginning of iniquity found in Lucifer, the Devil. Note Ezekiel 28:15: "Thou [both Adam and the Devil] *wast* perfect in thy ways from the day that thou wast created, till iniquity was found in thee."

> I John 3:9:
> Whosoever is born of God doth not commit sin [in the spirit]; for his [God's] seed [Christ] remaineth in him [the man]: and he cannot sin [in that of which he is born, the seed of God, Christ in him], because he is born of God.

In this seed of which a man is born again, he cannot sin. It is perfect spiritual seed.

> Verse 10:
> In this the children of God are manifest, and the children of the devil: whosoever doeth not righteousness is not of God, neither he that loveth not his brother.

Note the sharp line of demarcation between the two spiritual seeds. The children follow the pattern of their respective fathers.

Verses 11 and 12:
For this is the message that ye heard from
the beginning, that we should love one
another.

Not as Cain, *who* was of that wicked one,
and slew his brother. And wherefore slew
he him? Because his own works were evil,
and his brother's righteous.

Cain was "of that wicked one"; he was born
of the seed of the serpent and manifested the
Devil's hate and evil works.

Verses 13 and 14:
Marvel not, my brethren, if the world hate
you.

We know that we have passed from death
unto life, because we love the brethren. He
that loveth not *his* brother abideth in death.

The word "brethren" has the connotation of
"saints" as sons of God. We know that we have
passed from death unto life when our deeds are
motivated by the love of God. Our salvation is
manifested to ourselves and to the other saints
as we love with the love of God in our renewed
minds. No one has this *agapē* love until he is

born again of God. The natural man at best can only have *philia,* human love.

In the last part of verse 14 the words "*his* brother" are not in the oldest texts. "He that loveth not" refers to the unsaved man. The unsaved person cannot love with *agapē* love and remains in darkness.

> Verse 15:
> Whosoever hateth his brother is a murderer: and ye know that no murderer hath eternal life abiding in him.

Some churches have taught that anyone who commits murder, one who actually takes another's life, does not have eternal life abiding in him. The Word of God does not say this. "Whosoever hateth [hate is of the Devil, and only the Devil's children can have it] his brother [in the flesh] is a murderer...." The brother is not killed, but the man who hates, who is born of the seed of the serpent, is causing his own death. "...No murderer [who causes his own death because he is born of the seed of the serpent] hath eternal life abiding in him." He cannot have eternal life; he is born of the serpent.

Verse 16:
Hereby perceive [understand] we the love *of God,* because he [Jesus Christ] laid down his life for us: and we ought to lay down *our* lives for the brethren [saints].

We ought to lay down our lives, put our selfish desires in subjection to our spirit, to help our fellow believers.

Verse 17:
But whoso hath this world's good, and seeth his brother [saint] have need, and shutteth up his bowels *of compassion* from him, how dwelleth the love of God in him?

We have frequently been taught that we are to help the unsaved who are starving. This scripture tells us that our primary responsibility is to our brothers in Christ.*

Verses 18-22:
My little children, let us not love in word, neither in tongue; but in deed and in truth [Let us love and not just talk about it].

---

*Galatians 6:10: "As we have therefore opportunity, let us do good unto all *men,* especially unto them who are of the household of faith."

And hereby we know that we are of the truth, and shall assure our hearts before him [God].

For if our heart condemn us, God is greater than our heart, and knoweth all things.

Beloved, if our heart condemn us not, *then* have we confidence toward God.

And whatsoever we ask, we receive of him [God], because we keep [in our minds] his [God's] commandments, and do [in our actions] those things that are pleasing in his [God's] sight.

If our hearts are condemning us, we are out of fellowship with God. We have sinned by not walking in the renewed mind. When we are out of fellowship, we have no confidence toward God, and we cannot get our prayers answered.

Verse 23:
And this is his [God's] commandment, That we should believe on the name of his Son Jesus Christ, and love one another, as he [God in Christ Jesus] gave us commandment.

We can stake our very lives on the goodness which God has provided for us if we practice His will. Here we have a command, not a demand; we should believe on the name of His Son, Jesus Christ. Jesus, the firstborn, and we, his brethren, are to manifest the love from the Father within His family.

> Verse 24:
> And he that keepeth his commandments dwelleth in him [God], and he [God] in him. And hereby we know that he [God] abideth in us, by the Spirit which he hath given us.

The person who keeps the commandments not only has sonship but also fellowship. We can know that God in Christ dwells in us by manifesting the spirit which He has given to us.

> I John 4:1-3:
> Beloved, believe not every spirit, but try the spirits whether they are of God: because many false prophets are gone out into the world.
>
> Hereby know ye the Spirit of God: Every spirit that confesseth that Jesus Christ is come in the flesh is of God:

> And every spirit that confesseth not that Jesus Christ is come in the flesh is not of God: and this is that *spirit* of antichrist, whereof ye have heard that it should come; and even now already is it in the world.

We are not to believe every supernatural manifestation but are to test the spirits whether they be from the true God. To do this we need to operate the manifestation of discerning of spirits. The spirit of a false prophet will not be able to confess that Jesus Christ is come in the flesh. The same is antichrist but not *the* Antichrist.

> Verse 4:
> Ye are of God, little children, and have overcome them: because greater is he [God in Christ] that is in you, than he [the Devil and his devil spirits] that is in the world.

God in Christ in us, the holy spirit, is greater than the spirits of the Devil in the world. When we believers begin to practice our legal sonship rights with the use of the name of Jesus Christ, we will truly live with power and will overcome the forces of Satan in our lives.

Verses 5-12:

They [antichrists] are of the world: therefore speak they of the world, and the world heareth them.

We are of God: he that knoweth God heareth us; he that is not of God heareth not us. Hereby know we the spirit of truth [God], and the spirit of error [a devil spirit].

Beloved, let us love one another: for love is of God; and every one that loveth is born of God, and knoweth God.

He that loveth not knoweth not God; for God is love.

In this was manifested the love of God toward us, because that God sent his only begotten Son into the world, that we might live through him.

Herein is love, not that we loved God, but that he loved us, and sent his Son *to be* the propitiation [payment] for our sins.

Beloved, if God so loved us, we ought also to love one another [with the renewed mind].

No man hath seen God at any time. If we love one another, God dwelleth in us, and his love is perfected in us.

No man has ever seen God, for God is Spirit. God's love is perfected in our walk as our minds are renewed.

> Verses 13-15:
> Hereby know we that we dwell in him [God], and he in us, because he hath given us of his Spirit [His gift, holy spirit].
>
> And we have seen and do testify that the Father sent the Son *to be* the Saviour of the world.
>
> Whosoever shall confess that Jesus is the Son of God, God dwelleth in him, and he in God.

When God dwells in a man, he has received a new creation, eternal life. When a man dwells in God, the man is walking in fellowship in the renewed mind.

> Verse 16:
> And we have known and believed the love that God hath to us. God is love [*agapē*]; and he that dwelleth in love [*agapē*] dwelleth in God, and God in him.

God's love is perfected in our minds to the extent that we dwell in God and thereby manifest His gift to the world.

Verse 17:
Herein is our love made perfect, that we
may have boldness in the day of judgment:
because as he [God] is, so are we in this
world.

As God is, so are we who are born again and
who demonstrate love. We then have boldness
and power in a time of crisis, for we have put
on the armor of God.

Verses 18 and 19:
There is no fear in love; but perfect love
casteth out fear: because fear hath torment.
He that feareth is not made perfect in love.

We love him, because he first loved us.

God first loved us and gave us eternal life
which made it possible for us to love (*agapē*).
Now we ought to renew our minds according to
the Spirit, God, and walk before Him in love.

Verses 20 and 21:
If a man say, I love God, and hateth his
brother, he is a liar: for he that loveth not
his brother whom he hath seen, how can he
love God whom he hath not seen?

And this commandment have we from him,
That he who loveth God love his brother
also.

"To hate," as in this scripture, is "not to love."
The proof to ourselves and others that we love
God is to manifest the love of God to the saints.

I John 5:1:
Whosoever believeth that Jesus is the Christ
is born of God: and every one that loveth
him [God] that begat loveth him [Christ and
the brethren] also that is begotten of him.

Everyone who loves God in the renewed mind
loves the brethren, for it is impossible to have
the love of God in the renewed mind without
loving the brethren. Both Christ and we are
begotten of God. Christ is our brother, and we
are all, along with him, God's children.

Verse 2:
By this we know that we love the children
of God, when we love God, and keep his
commandments.

261

We keep His commandments by renewing our minds according to His Word. As we walk in this light, we prove to ourselves that we are the children of God.

> Verses 3 and 4:
> For this is the love of God, that we keep his [God's] commandments: and his commandments are not grievous [burdensome].
>
> For whatsoever is born of God overcometh the world: and this is the victory that overcometh the world [Satan], *even* our faith.

The word "world" refers to Satan throughout this epistle. The world includes all of Satan's realm and the things in it. We have the God-given ability to overcome all oppression because "greater is he that is in you, than he that is in the world." Our victory comes with (1) our believing in the Word of God and (2) renewing our minds according to it.

> Verse 5:
> Who is he that overcometh the world, but he that believeth that Jesus is the Son of God?

Jesus overcame the world, and the same power belongs to us as we minister and operate the manifestations of the spirit.*

> Verses 6-8:
>
> This is he that came by water and blood, *even* Jesus Christ; not by water only, but by water and blood. And it is the Spirit that beareth witness [with our spirit, the inner man], because the Spirit is truth.
>
> For there are three that bear record in heaven, the Father, the Word, and the Holy Ghost: and these three are one.
>
> And there are three that bear witness in earth, the Spirit, and the water, and the blood: and these three agree in one.**

According to verse 6, Jesus Christ came by water and blood. We know that Jesus was conceived in Mary by the Holy Spirit. At the time

---

*John 14:12: "Verily, verily, I say unto you, He that believeth on me, the works that I do shall he do also; and greater *works* than these shall he do; because I go unto my Father."

**According to the critical Greek text, the following words were first added in verses 7 and 8 in the sixteenth century: "...in heaven, the Father, the Word, and the Holy Ghost: and these three are one. And there are three that bear witness in earth...."

of Jesus' birth, the amniotic sac surrounding the fetus was broken and therefore water came forth. Blood also comes forth at birth with the mother's delivery of the child. Thus Jesus "came by water and blood," just as all of us do.

I, too, by natural birth, was born of water and blood. But the spirit within me, which came at the time of my spiritual birth, indicates that I am no longer just a natural man, for I have eternal life which is spirit. These three—water, blood, and spirit—witness to the same God Who was witnessed to when Jesus was born.

> Verses 9-12:
>
> If we receive the witness of men [regarding our birth of blood and water], the witness of God is greater: for this is the witness of God which he hath testified of his Son.
>
> He that believeth on the Son of God hath the witness in himself: he that believeth not God hath made him [God] a liar; because he believeth not the record that God gave of his Son.
>
> And this is the record, that God hath given to us eternal life, and this life is in his Son.
>
> He that hath the Son hath life; *and* he that hath not the Son of God hath not life.

When we believed on the Son of God, we received the witness of eternal life within. "He that hath the Son hath life," according to the text. We do not earn this life given to us by God; we do not beg for it; we cannot steal it; and we cannot lose it, because God gave it to us as seed.

> Verses 13 and 14:
> These things have I written unto you that believe on the name of the Son of God; that ye may know that ye have eternal life, and that ye may believe on the name of the Son of God.
>
> And this is the confidence that we have in him, that, if we ask any thing according to his will, he heareth us.

However, by the same token, if we ask anything which is not God's will, we will receive nothing. We must know His will in order to know what properly and rightfully to ask for.

> Verse 15:
> And if we know that he hear us, whatsoever we ask, we know that we have [present tense] the petitions that we desired [past tense] of him.

We have our requests before we have the manifestation of them. This is tremendous. Why? The Bible is the Word of God, and the Word of God is the will of God. Therefore, if we know the Word of God, we know the will of God. If the Word says, "Pray for the sick," then we know that we are to pray for the sick; we are doing God's will. We need no longer pray the pitiful "If it be Thy will." Only someone unlearned or ignorant of the Word of God will pray "If it be Thy will." The man who knows the Word of God knows what is God's will.

> Verse 16:
> If any man see his brother sin a sin *which is* not unto death, he shall ask, and he shall give him life for them that sin not unto death. There is a sin unto death: I do not say that he shall pray for it.

The "sin unto death" is the unforgivable sin. (See "The Unforgivable Sin," *The Word's Way,* chapter 4.) If a man commits this sin, prayer will avail nothing, for that man is born of the seed of the serpent. However, if a brother in the flesh has not committed the unforgivable sin, God will give that brother eternal life if we ask. The word "brother" in verse 16 specifically refers to a brother by birth. We can pray for salvation for a family member who wills to hear and believe God's promise. Praying for eternal life for a relative, brother or sister, who has not committed the unforgivable sin is a key which we can lay hold on for members of our families who are not saved.

Verse 17:
All unrighteousness is sin: and there is a sin not unto death.

Anything in thought, word, or deed which is not in harmony with God's Word is unrighteousness. The unrighteousness of those who are born again is not unto death because God has promised forgiveness.

Verse 18:
We know that whosoever is born of God sinneth not [in the spirit, inner man]; but he that is begotten of God keepeth himself, and that wicked one toucheth him not.

If this verse were translated, "We know that which is born of God within the believer sinneth not," people could understand more easily. "Whosoever is born of God" remains in fellowship with God by renewing his mind. The believer with a renewed mind cannot be touched by the wicked one. The key to keeping ourselves is in living according to God's Word. By positive action we will allow no opportunity for Satan to interfere in our lives. As Ephesians 4:27 admonishes, "Neither give place to the devil."

> I John 5:19 and 20:
> *And* we know that we are of God, and the whole world lieth in wickedness.
>
> And we know that the Son of God is come, and hath given us an understanding, that we may know him that is true, and we are in him that is true, *even* in his Son Jesus Christ. This is the true God, and eternal life.

The whole world *lies,* not walks or stands but *lies,* helpless as a babe or a dead body, before the wicked one, Satan. He is the prince of this world, according to John 14:30, and the god of this world, according to II Corinthians 4:4. However, we who are born again have been enlightened, for we know God Who is true.

I John 5:21:
Little children, keep yourselves from idols.
Amen.

"Little children" is a term of endearment, as
to students from a concerned and loving teacher.
To "keep from idols" means to seek no help,
guidance, or instruction from any source other
than our heavenly Father, Who is the true and
living God. We should not be swayed from keeping our minds on God and His Word. Our victorious living, after receiving sonship, comes in
direct proportion with our remaining in fellowship by thinking and acting according to the will
of God, which can only be known by the Word
of God.

269

Scripture Index

About the Author

Victor Paul Wierwille spent several decades vigorously and prayerfully searching out the truths of God's Word. As part of his search he consulted and worked with many outstanding individuals in Christian studies for keys to power-filled, victorious living. Such men as Karl Barth, Joseph Bauer, Glenn Clark, Karl J. Ernst, Josiah Friedli, Louis C. Hessert, Elmer G. Homrighausen, E. Stanley Jones, George M. Lamsa, Richard and Reinhold Niebuhr, K.C. Pillai, Paul Tillich, Ernst Traeger, and many others were a part of Dr. Wierwille's quest to find the truths of the Word of God.

Dr. Wierwille's academic career included Bachelor of Arts and Bachelor of Theology degrees from Mission House (Lakeland) College and Seminary, graduate studies at the University of Chicago and at Princeton Theological Seminary, where he earned the Master of Theology degree in Practical Theology. Later he completed his work for the Doctor of Theology degree at Pikes Peak Bible Seminary and Burton College in Manitou Springs, Colorado.

For over forty years, Dr. Wierwille devoted his major energies to intensive research and teaching of the accuracy of God's Word. In 1953 he began teaching his Biblical research in classes on Power for Abundant Living. He was the founder and first president of The Way International, a non-sectarian, nondenominational Biblical research, teaching, and fellowship ministry. He held the presidency of The Way College of Emporia, and he was the founder and first president of several other centers of learning: The Way College of Biblical Research, Indiana Campus; Camp Gunnison; and LEAD Outdoor Academy International.

As Dr. Wierwille persevered in his research of the Bible, he continued to write more research works and to develop further classes in Biblical studies, including The University of Life outreach courses, an international Biblical studies correspondence school. As a dynamic lecturer, he traveled and taught worldwide, holding forth the greatness and the accuracy of God's Word with great intensity until his death in May of 1985.

280